The Man Who is Mrs. Brown

David O'Dornan

JOHN BLAKE

Published by John Blake Publishing Ltd,
3 Bramber Court, 2 Bramber Road,
London W14 9PB, England

www.johnblakepublishing.co.uk

www.facebook.com/Johnblakepub facebook
twitter.com/johnblakepub twitter

First published in paperbackback in 2013

ISBN: 978-1-78219-494-1

British Library Cataloguing in Publication Data:

A catalogue record for this book is available from the British Library.

Design by www.envydesign.co.uk

Printed in Great Britain by CPI Group (UK) Ltd

1 3 5 7 9 10 8 6 4 2

Papers used by John Blake Publishing are natural, recyclable
products made from wood grown in sustainable forests.
The manufacturing processes conform to the environmental
regulations of the country of origin.

Every attempt has been made to contact the relevant copyright-holders,
but some were unobtainable. We would be grateful if the appropriate
people could contact us.

This book is dedicated to Tara.
My love, my wife, my life.

CONTENTS

ACKNOWLEDGEMENTS

To all of my family and dearest friends, you know who you are, and especially to my loving parents, mum Sandra and dad Alec, my wife's family, big brother Mark and my wife Tara, a marvellous 'mammy' in her own right to our beautiful children, Lexi and Charlie. Thank you for your patience, love and support while I worked on this book.

Sincere thanks goes to Rosie Virgo from John Blake Publishing for her faith in me as she approached me to write the book and her former colleague Sara Cywinski who suggested the book to her employers in the first place and offered me great encouragement and advice.

Warm thanks too to those who agreed to be interviewed for the book: Gerry Browne, Gay Byrne, Tommy Swarbrigg and Adele King, and to Gerry and my employers Independent News & Media for picture assistance. Special thanks must go to my brilliant book editor Rodney Burbeck for his invaluable skills as well as his patience and understanding with this being my first book. He's been a great teacher.

And finally to Brendan O'Carroll, for though he does not know it unless he is reading this now, but he has been an unforeseen but incredible influence on my life. I hope I have done justice to his amazing life story and it proves to be an inspiration to others.

David O'Dornan, 2013

CHAPTER 1

CHILD OF DESTINY

Lying in a pool of blood on a Dublin street, wounded after being shot, lies a young boy. He has only a slight pulse. Beside him, his father lies dead.

They were shot by British officers from the Black and Tans, World War One veteran British soldiers sent in 1920 to assist the Royal Irish Constabulary as the Irish War of Independence became a brutal and bloody affair. They were targeted because they were Republicans. Dragged from their family shop and frogmarched out onto the street, they were placed on their knees and the soldiers demanded information. When they refused, the officers cocked their rifles and pulled the triggers.

The shopkeeper was shot three times and killed instantly, while the little boy was hit once in the shoulder. His life

was ebbing away, except the boy, just nine years old, didn't
die. A journalist who came upon the scene saved his life by
carrying him to the nearby Richmond Hospital. That
young boy was Gerard O'Carroll.

The next day, over breakfast, the journalist recounted the
story to his family including his eight-year-old daughter
Maureen. As fate would have it, Maureen grew up to fall in
love with Gerard, the boy whose life her father saved, and
they would have 11 children – the last to arrive being a
certain Brendan O'Carroll.

Brendan's grandfather Peter and his adult sons were in
the Irish Republican Army which emerged after the Easter
Rising. They were a different animal from the Provisional
IRA paramilitary organisation that would wreak havoc
from 1969 onwards in The Troubles, but nonetheless they
were still an armed revolutionary military outfit.

Revealing the story of his dramatic family background to
interviewer Barbara Bogaev on Washington radio
programme *Fresh Air* on National Public Radio, when he
was promoting his novels in the States in the spring of 1999,
Brendan stressed that the old IRA were a kind of Republican
army, and his grandfather would have been a covert operator
– 'a commando, for the want of a better word'.

'He owned a small store – a kind of a drugstore, candy
and cigarette store – in Manor Street in Dublin. And
although he was quite safe and his cover hadn't ever been
blown, his three eldest sons, my father's three eldest
brothers, were active soldiers. They weren't covert soldiers.
And they were well-known.

'This British contingent came around to the house at
7pm one evening and said, "Look, we want to know where

your three sons are." And what he would do is he'd lead them into the store while he was putting on his boots, they'd help themselves to a pack of cigarettes or a couple of sticks of candy and then leave.

'He was putting on his boots and they said, "You know, we're coming back tonight. And if you don't have the information where your sons are, we'll kill you." He took it with a grain of salt. And they arrived back at about 10pm and the three sons were upstairs. When they heard the banging on the door, the sons escaped onto the roof and started to make their way across the rooftops and to get out of the area.

'My dad, who was nine at the time, he went down with his father. They didn't even give [my grandfather] a chance to put his boots on. He opened the door, and they said, "Kneel down." And they put a gun to his head and they said, "So where are three boys?" And he said, "I don't know. And if I knew, I wouldn't tell you."

'And they said, "Are you Sinn Fein?" And he said, "Born, and I'll die." And they said, "Then die." And they shot him three times – once in the head, once in the chest, and one in the stomach. And then they shot my father... and left him for dead.'

Brendan says he still has newspaper cuttings of the time, reporting the killings detailing how the soldiers pinned a notice to his shirt when he was lying on the ground that said, "This man is a traitor to the Queen..."

Another press report, a treasured keepsake of his family history, told how his grandmother, who was upstairs, was afraid to come down. 'It is so illuminating,' he says. 'It read "Mrs O'Carroll, fearful for her life, retired to her bedroom

3

THE MAN WHO IS MRS. BROWN

and betook herself to prayer." Isn't that lovely? Isn't that charming? You wouldn't see that in the press nowadays.'

The circumstances of his father's survival and marriage to the daughter of his rescuer, is an extraordinary twist of fate that determined the existence of one of the biggest showbiz stars Ireland has ever produced. But Brendan's formidable mother, Maureen, who would become the first woman elected to the Irish parliament, also had fate to thank for her own existence.

Her parents were all set to elope to America and had tickets bought for the ill-fated *Titanic*, only for a change of plan at the eleventh hour. Brendan shared the remarkable tale during that same Washington radio station interview in 1999:

'The story was that my mam's mother made an announcement that she was about to marry a man who actually was older than her own father. She was 18 at the time, and this guy was 44. And her father wasn't having any of it. He said absolutely no way was he having any piece of this. So they decided in secret that they would elope. And my grandmother over a couple of weeks, little by little, snuck her clothes out of the house. And when she had them all ready and all out, she was ready to go away and go to America.

'They were going to elope to America, which in that time, I'm talking about early 1900s, eloping to America meant never coming home. There was no four-hour, five-hour flights home. So she sat up the night before she was to leave, and was quite upset about her father, who she was at this stage probably really fighting with.

'The thought of saying goodbye to her mother the next day, with her mother thinking she was just going to work and never seeing her mother again, was very upsetting to her. While she was sitting up in the kitchen of the home, her mother came down and said, "Are you OK?" And she said, "Yeah, I'm OK."

'So they made two cups of hot milk. And they sat there sipping hot milk. And in the middle of the conversation, my grandmother eventually told her mother what she doing, that she was eloping to America. Her mother said, "Look, if your dad knew you were this serious, he would relent and you could have a proper marriage here in Ireland." So she convinced my grandmother to wake up her father, which she did.

'And he threw the head. He went bananas. I mean, he went berserk, but then calmed down and agreed that rather than elope they should get married here in Ireland. My grandmother went around, told her boyfriend, who was delighted, and he went down to Heuston Station in Dublin that day to sell the tickets that he'd bought for the elopement. The tickets were to get the train to Cobh in Ireland, at that time it was called Queenstown, to pick up the *Titanic* heading for the United States of America. He sold the tickets to a newly graduated police officer and his wife who just got married. And they went away – they were going away on a break. And he sold them to him.'

There's another extraordinary ironic twist of fate in this tale coming up, as Brendan explained: 'Fast forward 35 years and my mam is heading a police commission to try and establish a women's police force in Ireland, and the first in Europe.

'At that time, the attitude was women can work in the police force, but only, you know, as secretaries and whatever, but not in uniform. And she wanted to establish an Irish women's police force. She was up against a board of police chiefs, one particular hard nut guy. A real hard nut. He wasn't having any of it.

'After work one Friday evening, she was walking through Stephen's Green [in central Dublin]. She bumped into this police chief. It had been a pretty acrimonious day, so the conversation was kind of stand-offish. So he said, "Good night, safe home." And she said, "I'm not going home, I'm going over to the Shelbourne Hotel, where I'm going to have a scotch on the rocks. And I'm going to tell the waiter to keep bringing it until I can't pronounce it."

'So the policeman laughed and he said, "Well, maybe I'll join you for one or two." So she said OK. So they started walking together. And on the way, she said, "There's a telephone in the hotel. You can ring your wife and tell her you'll be late."

'He said, "I'm a widower." She said, "I'm sorry to hear that. Is your wife long dead?"

"Well," he said, "actually, she drowned on the *Titanic*. I was lucky to have survived. But she didn't make it."

'And my mother stopped and said, "Did you buy the tickets off a gentleman named McHugh?" And he said, "Yes, I did." And she said, "That was my dad."

'So they went into the Shelbourne, had copious amounts of scotch. And the next day, history records, the Ban Gardai [the Irish Women's Police Force] was founded.'

With such a remarkable family history like this, it was clear that Brendan O'Carroll was born to be different.

CHAPTER 2

THE RUNT OF THE LITTER

He has now become a global phenomenon with his award-winning TV show *Mrs Brown's Boys*, but Brendan O'Carroll's life story to date is no ordinary tale of a man intent on a career in showbiz. With his roots in rough-and-tumble working class areas of Dublin, Brendan confesses it's a minor miracle he didn't instead embark on a life of crime and prison.

He was, as he says, 'the runt of the litter', the eleventh child his remarkable mother Maureen gave birth to, with his cries first being heard in Dublin on 15 September 1955. He was born when she was 46 and a sitting parliamentarian.

Speaking to presenter Jacki Lyden from National Public Radio in the US, Brendan said his mother told him he was 'one more time, for old time's sake, and she was probably right'.

'When I was 13,' he went on, 'I found her diary and on the 5th of December, 1951, she had written, "I must see Dr Kearney. He says I'm either pregnant or it's a growth." And in brackets she had added, "I hope it's a growth." So she wished me well!

'That was me. I was the growth. So I found this and said "look what you wrote" and she said, "I know and ye are a growth – and you were malignant!" Anyway, she was quite an extraordinary woman.'

Dublin, for those not familiar with it, can be loosely divided into two classes separated by the River Liffey – the poor, working class north side and the more affluent south side. The O'Carrolls lived on the north side in an area called Stoneybatter, which nestles between the market area of Smithfield with its Jameson Whiskey distillery and Phoenix Park, one of the largest walled city parks in Europe. In Brendan's childhood days, at the top of Stoneybatter on the North Circular Road, they held the city's cattle market.

'The house where I was born is in an area called the Cowtown, where all the cattle came to be put up for auction,' Brendan told the *Evening Times*. 'I can remember the hundreds of cows filling the streets, right outside the doors. In fact, each of the houses has a little built-in shoe scraper block.'

Their little two-up, two-down house was home to Brendan, his five sisters and five brothers, and parents Gerard and Maureen. He jokes that, 'Mum slept with the girls, Dad slept with the boys. How they had 11 kids is beyond me. They must have had an extension cord.'

He went to the St Gabriel's National School, just round the corner from the house, until he was 12, when he left to get a job. Now, he sponsors the schoolkids writing journals.

'Later, when I appeared in the movie *Angela's Ashes*, I played the undertaker and had to drive a hearse up the very street where I was born. As for Cowtown, it's now the fashionable place to live. It's full of journalists and lawyers.'

Maureen O'Carroll was such an inspiration to her devoted son Brendan – he idolised her but lived in fear as much as awe. Awe because she was such a special 'extraordinary' woman, and she doted on the baby of her brood; fear that he would not disappoint her, and it was only after she died that he summoned the courage to try his hand at showbiz. Brendan's father Gerard, despite the bloody drama of his childhood, grew up a quiet man and was a cabinet maker.

But Brendan's childhood was to change when his family were forced to move from inner-city Dublin to Finglas, a suburb to the north of the city – a move that would later form part of the plot in his book *The Chisellers*, the second in the Agnes Browne trilogy. And in the introduction to the 1998 book *Finglas – A Celebration*, he recounted his memories of the move:

It was a big dark green rickety old Leyland bus that took us on our very first trip to Finglas. Dublin Corporation, in its wisdom, decided to move a few hundred families from the inner city to the new suburbs. Finglas! We had never heard of the place.

This was the end of the world as we knew it. Beyond

this – as far as we were concerned – were wild animals, and forests, and places that my father would threaten to take us and leave us if we didn't behave. Now, believe it or not, here we were going voluntarily to live!

That year was 1960. I was just five years old. What I thought then to be the end of my world as I knew it instead began the most wonderful and adventurous time of my life – childhood in Finglas. It became easy, and it's still easy, for the newspapers to headline the misdoings of the Finglas area, for they were easier to write, required little research except police reports, and made better headlines than anything positive that might be going on in the Finglas area.

However, there are a handful of people who received no credit, or headlines, and were responsible for the transformation of our area and our young people. They were the volunteers. The people who really made up the community.

It was these people who ran the Street League Football. It was these people who ran the Community Games. It was these people who gave us the majorettes of Finglas South. Ordinary men and women who, after a day's work, would either cycle or bus their way back to Finglas and spend their evenings running youth clubs, football clubs or athletic clubs.

I look back now on the work of those people, those unsung heroes, and know in my heart that without any shadow of a doubt it was the hard work of these people who kept myself, and the likes of me, out of prison.

I'm from Finglas and I'm proud of it!

Proud he is now, but when his family, like hundreds of others, were first decanted out of the city it seemed there was almost zero amenities, no work and no hope.

'The town had no amenities,' Brendan told the *Evening Times*, 'just a bog field where we could play football but then one day the Corporation built a swimming pool, the Cabra Baths. Nowadays there are €5million leisure centres in the area. But this pool was open air, just a big hole in the ground and it was filled with freezing river water. But we loved it, as it was somewhere to go. We all had horses when we were kids here. We'd ride them around the streets.'

There was little else to do. Many of his childhood pals would end up in jail – or dead. But Brendan has always been a survivor. He's had more than his fair share of heartache in his life, and the death of his father was his first. His dad Gerard died from asbestos poisoning when Brendan was just nine years old: 'He died in the same hospital where they took him when he had been shot as a kid,' says Brendan.

In his father's final days, Brendan remembers being given a half-crown to buy two pigeons, which as a child he was fond of collecting. 'I told Dad I was keeping them in pop soda crates and he said "When I get out of here, I'll build you the best pigeon loft in the country." He died the next week and when Mum told me I asked, "But what about my loft?"

Brendan has few memories of his father, although he does recall being rocked on his knee as they watched television together: 'I remember that fondly, how lovely that was,' Brendan told Irish broadcaster and friend Gay Byrne on his RTE television show *The Meaning of Life*.

'He thought he had a bad back and took the door off the coal shed and put it under his mattress, because it gave him some relief. He was only 55 when he died.' Times were hard and he had plenty to cope with at a young age, but Brendan remembers 'laughter, a lot of laughter. We were poor, but we weren't unhappy.'

The seeds of Brendan's belief in PMA – Positive Mental Attitude – were sown during his childhood, as he told the *Irish Mirror*:

We didn't have a lot of money when I was a kid. There were 11 children, Dad was a cabinetmaker and Mammy was a TD [the Irish equivalent of an MP] who was out a lot saving the world. It was Mammy I got my positive energy from. She taught me to believe in myself. With Dad she showed me you have to work hard to make things work.

As a youngster I was known as St Anthony because of my knack of finding anything that was lost. I would imagine the lost item in my mind's eye and simply walk over and find it. It's a fantastic ability. I can still do it today.

The first time I remember it happening was when I was six. I was at the beach with Mammy, an aunt and a load of my cousins. My aunt was paddling with a couple of her kids and she was grabbing big wet handfuls of sand, but when she came back to our rug where the rest of us were she noticed she had lost her wedding ring.

It was one of the only bits of jewellery she had and

she was devastated at losing it. But Mammy told her not to worry because I would find it. It seemed a daft idea that I could find a ring that was lost on a huge beach but Mammy was convinced. We walked to where my aunt thought she had been. I put my hands into the wet sand and as I pulled them up, her wedding ring was dangling off my little finger. She couldn't believe it but I didn't think it was any big deal.

A year later I was to learn one of the other most important things in my life – the power of negative thought and the consequences that can have. Dad died that year – because I believe he wanted to. He was a great man but not in touch with his emotions.

So when Mammy became ill he couldn't cope so he wished himself dead – and he died. Some people think that's a strange idea, but it's not. Learning the lessons of positive and negative thought helped me as I grew up.

His father's death while he was still a kid left Brendan under the sole influence of his mother, Maureen, who instilled in him a sense of independence, despite the fact that her own life seemed to be a mass of contradictions.

'My mother had a degree, my mother was a secondary school teacher, my mother was a Labour TD, and this is where you find a huge difference if you look across my family,' Brendan told *The Irish Times*.

'I can sit down with members of my family and they talk about a woman I don't know when they talk about my mother, and I talk about a woman that they don't know when I talk about my mother. My older sisters remember her as a woman they would hear on the radio, decrying the fact that so many children were coming out of primary school illiterate, yet she wouldn't be there to help them with their homework.

'A woman with a degree who fought for free education, and yet not one of her 11 children went past primary education. Well, I think that's an indictment of her.

'I didn't see that side of her. I got the best of her, because the only saving grace for me was that, when my dad died, my mam retired from politics. And at that stage, most of my brothers and sisters had each moved out, married or emigrated.

'So I was left with the undivided attention of this complete genius who used to sit me on the table when I was seven, tie my shoelaces and then look me in the eyes and say to me, "You know, you can be anything you want to be." And I believed her. I grew up believing I can be anything I want to be. She had tremendous belief in independence.'

But with so much turmoil in his young life, maybe it's no surprise that Brendan ended up in trouble with the law: when he was nine he was caught shoplifting. It saw him before the courts, and sentenced to three months at Daingean Reformatory in Co Offaly, a youth detention centre. His mum was furious. She was determined that he be taught a lesson – so he went to the borstal, even though she had the power to spare him.

He told the *Irish Times*: 'I remember when I was caught stealing in Superquinn supermarket, she had enough clout to get the charges pulled but she said, "Did you do it?" and I said, "Yeah" and she said, "Well, the best of luck in court."

'It was my ninth birthday and I was sent away to

Daingean [children's reformatory]. She could have stopped all that but her attitude was, if you do something well, you stand on the roofs tops and say, "Look at this! I did this!" But you've got to do that when things don't go well – "Hey, look, I'm sorry. I did it, it was me." And d'you know, there's an incredible freedom in doing that.

'Mum used to boast that she had 11 children but had never stood in a courtroom with any of them, and then I let her down.'

Brendan told Gay Byrne more about his experience on *The Meaning of Life*: "I was the worst thief in the world. It was a roll of Sellotape, a bicycle lock, two Oxo cubes and a Biro. I had this stuff and I looked – there's the door, there's me. Door, me. And I nearly made it. It was very peculiar the way it ended up, because I didn't think I would get punished for it, I didn't think my mother thought I'd get punished for something like that, she thought that I'd maybe go to court, get probation and that it would scare the living daylights out of me.

'But I'm not sure that the judge and herself had in the past politically seen eye to eye, and they thought that a period of minding might do me the world of good.

'I arrived and when I was being checked in, the Brother that was checking me in asked me when was the last time I got mass. I said "yesterday morning". "And before that?" he asked. "The morning before that," I said. "I can serve the mass in Latin." And he said, "You can serve the mass in Latin?"

'Well, I became a star. In Daingean I was a star. I served mass every day and I was minded, without a shadow of a doubt I was treated softly because of that. Some of the guys there had terrible times.'

Brendan was lucky to get an easy ride at Daingean, but he still had to run the gauntlet while he was still a little boy attending St Gabriel's Boys National School. He remembers how strict and violent schools were in those days.

'The Brother had a belt with the "Wrath of God" written across it,' he told the *Irish Mirror*. 'You would get caned six or 12 times – it was very severe. It was absolutely terrifying to be in a classroom with him. It was like letting a psycho loose in the class. It's sick that those belts and canes were made specifically for beating little children.'

But there was one teacher who had a more profound influence on Brendan, as he told the *Irish Sunday Mirror*: 'Billy Flood, one of my old school teachers brought an empty Tayto crisps box full of books in one day and started a library.

'The first book I borrowed was *Treasure Island*. I read it four times and when I was leaving school he gave me the book. He had written inside: "I stood and looked and my wonder grew that such a small head could hold all that he knew." Billy was the guest of honour at my first book launch.'

After school – rather than rush home as his mother would have him working chores at the woman's refuge she had set up – Brendan would rather be hanging around Moore Street, Dublin's open air fruit and vegetable market that, along with its market stall vendors, is a Dublin institution. Young Brendan would run errands for the women who ran the stalls. And they, he says, would be the biggest influence for his most enduring and money-spinning creation, Agnes Browne, [we'll hear later how and why the final 'e' was dropped] the 'mammy' of *Mrs Brown's Boys*.

By now Brendan – known as 'Boc' to his pals as a nickname, made from his initials – was growing up fast and was also discovering girls. He had his first kiss at the tender age of 10 with a girl called Mardi Deegan.

Reminiscing to the *Irish Sunday Mirror* he said: 'God love her... it happened in the middle of winter. I had what I used to call Number 11 – two lines of snot running from my nose. I took Mardi to the cinema and all the other boys were waiting to see if she would kiss me. Well she did and it was a big smack. I remember thinking, "I hope my nose is clean," but when she pulled away there was two silver spots on her upper lip – I had made my mark. Everyone saw it but no one told her – surprisingly enough she still speaks to me today.'

It can't be denied that Brendan was a rascal as a boy, like the time he set fire to the hedgerow at the back of his house and blamed it on his brother Michael. He confessed: 'My father was very proud of that hedgerow and he went mad when he saw it in flames. My brother was trying to put out the fire with a blanket and I had run away. He got the hiding of his life from our father and then our mother battered him for using a good blanket to put out the fire. I didn't own up until my 21st birthday.'

Often his partner in crime was his pal Gerry Browne. They mucked about as kids in Finglas and they would later reunite as adults to become partners on stage when Gerry proved instrumental in his early career.

Gerry recalls another fire-raising incident with Brendan when he was about 10: 'We bought two magnifying glasses,' he told the *Irish Sunday Mirror*, 'and decided to burn two holes in a display unit in a shop window in

Finglas village. We had this mad idea of burning holes in the eyes of the cockerel on the front of the Kellogg's Cornflakes box, but it just burst into flames. Five minutes later the fire brigade were breaking down the door to put out the fire. Thankfully, nobody was hurt, but I had a red bum and a sore ear for weeks as punishment.'

Gerry's mother Annie remembers first meeting a young Brendan when her two eldest sons, Gerry and Joey, started a band called Tinker's Fancy. Brendan didn't star in the band, rather he hung around with them, but Annie says there were clues to his ambition even back then.

Talking to Samantha Libreri for her book *Finglas: A People's Portrait*, she said: 'They used to all come in and have cups of tea and eat you outta house and home. Brendan was a real witty person, real funny. He always said he was going to write books and all that sort of thing. He was welcomed here and he was like, maybe you would say, part of the family.'

But Brendan's happiest childhood memory is playing football for Home Farm FC, a League of Ireland club on Dublin's north side that among others has produced Ireland internationals such as Johnny Carey and his fellow Manchester United star and Busby Babe, Liam 'Billy' Whelan, who died in the Munich Air Disaster, Liverpool's Ronnie Whelan, Manchester City's Richard Dunne and Leeds United's Gary Kelly.

Brendan was playing youth football at the same time future Arsenal star Liam Brady would have been learning his trade. Like any young boy he had dreams to be a professional footballer – but in later life he was just thankful to the club for keeping him out of trouble.

'[The club] was run by a group of local men who cycled to the pitch after a long day's work to try to put us into line. They kept us on the straight and narrow and got us interested in something that was good and healthy. They also taught us about team spirit and sportsmanship – we learned how to respect ourselves and others. I reckon that if it wasn't for this club I would have spent time in prison.'

CHAPTER 3

BRENDAN'S OWN MAMMY

It's a popular misconception that Brendan's most famous creation, Agnes Browne, later to drop the 'e' when *Mrs Brown's Boys* the stage play and TV series came along, is modelled on his mother, Maureen. She isn't entirely, but there is no doubt that, a formidable matriarch in her own right, Maureen was a tremendous influence on her boy, his life, and his works.

'All I wanted to do was impress me mam, that's all I ever wanted to do, to make me mam proud of me,' he confessed to Australian TV Channel Seven's current affairs programme *Sunday Night*. 'And one thing I knew I could do for sure was make her laugh. A lot of people ask is Mrs Brown based on my mum, I used to say no but I think somewhere along the lines she is, maybe my mum without the education.'

She, like Agnes and like Brendan himself, was a force of nature, an inspirational and impressive human being – and Brendan worshipped her. At an early age, Maureen decided on a life devoted to God, taking the first steps to becoming a nun. She started her training at Gortnor Abbey convent school in Co Mayo and then at University College Galway.

'She was quite an extraordinary woman,' says Brendan. 'She was a bibliophile, she absolutely adored books, and in the convent she found this perfect place where you could read in peace and quiet, and I think she confused that with a vocation.' When doubts began to creep into her thinking, and Maureen wanted to 'kick the habit' (as Brendan now jokes) she faced a two-year battle with Rome.

As Brendan put it in an interview with Gay Byrne on *The Meaning of Life*: 'Once she graduated from Galway University with her BA, she found out very quickly, "actually I wouldn't mind a bit of a man". So she did the right thing, but it was difficult for her.

'She was a nun right up to final vows. She was a nun for one year before she renounced her vows after she started to question her vocation and then had to fight the Vatican to get out of the convent. I mean, it was back in the forties and it was a tough time to be a woman. She had to fight to renounce her vows, and then had to go home and face the sticks and stones, because in Ireland at that time the only thing worse than not having a priest or a nun in your family was to have somebody who was in and was now out.

'And of course in hindsight, having 11 children later, obviously she was right to question her vocation. So she was a great battler. And she went on to be a tremendously strong and intelligent woman.'

It was to be only the first in a lifetime of fighting battles for Maureen. She became a secondary school teacher in Dublin, teaching languages, but was sacked because she got married – you couldn't hold a teaching position if you were a married woman at that time in Ireland. Ironically, this would lead to her forging a glittering career in politics. But she could never have imagined, back in Galway as a student nun, that she'd end up becoming the first female parliamentarian in Ireland.

She was so incensed at losing the teaching job for getting married, she said, "I'm not having that." She became involved in the union and got the ruling changed. 'She did such a good job that the Labour Party asked her to run for election for government,' says Brendan. 'In 1953, she became the only woman elected to the Irish Parliament. And she went on to become the first female minister of foreign affairs, the first female under-secretary of NATO (the North Atlantic Treaty Organisation).

'And she had 11 kids. The woman had a womb like a machine-gun. So she was quite an extraordinary woman for her time. She was an incredible woman.'

Brendan told TV host Miriam O'Callaghan on her *Saturday Night With Miriam* show on RTE in 2007 more about his mother's passion as a politician, particularly in campaigning for women's rights: 'She was a real go-getter. In many ways I got the benefit of that. She set about changing a lot of women's laws, some of them were ridiculous.

'One of the laws she changed was, at that time it was legal to beat your wife, provided you didn't use a stick longer than your forearm or thicker than your thumb. She got that changed. Up until 1992 it was legal to rape your wife.'

One of the first things Maureen did when she entered the Dáil [the Irish Parliament] was to lobby for the introduction of short birth certificates to get rid of the stigma of illegitimacy.

In an interview with Barbara Bogaev, on US radio channel Fresh Air, Brendan explained: 'The birth cert, if your father wasn't known, it said "bastard". So she got that changed, they changed it to "illegitimate". And the reason she was trying to do this is because when somebody went for a job in Ireland at that time, you had to have your birth certificate.

'Now as soon as the word bastard came up on your birth certificate, that was it. You didn't get the job. It was Holy Catholic Ireland. And they just didn't give you the job. So she wanted to get that removed to give everybody an equal chance of getting a job, regardless of what their parentage was. So eventually they got it changed to illegitimate.'

Among her other achievements towards women's rights was establishing the Ban Gardai in Ireland which saw women being allowed to serve as fully-fledged police officers. Before her intervention, the best women could hope for would be jobs in the police force as secretaries and cleaners. 'That was an incredible achievement and one I am very proud of,' says Brendan.

As the first female member of the Dáil at the age of 45, Maureen O'Carroll became known for her ability as an orator, often disarming opponents with humour and sarcasm. For her maiden speech in 1953, she chose to wear a trouser suit and was interrupted and criticised by the Speaker for her 'inappropriate' dress.

'Mr Speaker, I am the sitting member for Dublin North

Central and I'll wear a frock when every other deputy wears a frock,' was the curt reply. Brendan quite rightly loves telling that story and obviously adored the woman who was such an influence on him.

It's clear where Brendan gets his resolve from when you consider the determination of his mother, who despite a brood of 11 kids to raise in a cramped house and little money, still managed to achieve so much in her lifetime.

'My mother was a genius,' he says, beaming with pride. 'She gave me an overview, a direction. She taught me to think, so that I've never taken any aspect of life for granted. As the youngest I had her to myself. And she taught me how to grab whatever life has to offer.'

So you can be forgiven for assuming that Maureen O'Carroll also gave her son the prototype for Brendan's 'superstar' character, Mrs Brown (with or without an 'e'), who keeps her brood in line with a mix of approval, acerbic wit and the odd slap with a tea towel. And like Maureen, Agnes's underlying theme is always positive. She is always encouraging, always battling to make sure her kids turn out right.

'She was so far ahead of her time,' says Brendan. 'I feel sorry for her, because it must have been very frustrating for her. She was very much a woman's woman. Her life was all about making changes for the better. I have lived with that unbelievable legacy.'

It was her strength of character, her protective personality and, ironically, her death which made Brendan the man he is today. Brendan says his life moved from waiting tables and serving soup to screen success 'thanks' to his mother's death in 1984.

'This will sound completely mad,' he told the *Irish Sunday Mirror*, 'I loved my mother dearly – but the best thing she could have done for me was die. I could never express myself as an individual because I was always worried about whether she would approve. I have taken some incredible risks in my career, like becoming a stand-up comedian when my pub business went bust.

'But if my mother had been alive she would never have let the business go under and I would never have become a comedian. I have learned and lived more since my mother died because I have had some failures – lots of them.

'But despite that I loved her so much and it makes me really sad that she can't be here to see all of this. But I suppose she's up there somewhere looking down on me.

'All the same – I wish she could see me today – she would be very proud.

'I will always regret the fact that she has never seen me performing on stage or has read one of my books.

'My mother was a remarkable woman and I can't describe how much she has influenced me. We lived in a Corporation house ... any spare money was used for good causes. She opened a shelter for battered women with the money she made from politics and kept it going until she ran out of cash.

'Big, drunken men would come banging on the door, threatening her. And she'd just say: "Come on then, come on. I'll have you in prison so fast your feet won't touch the ground." And they'd back down.'

It's clear that Brendan remains intensely proud of his mum and has long held plans to write her biography based on the diaries she left him. Though his father was there throughout his childhood, he was a withdrawn figure, which Brendan describes as 'an absence'.

'My father was a cabinet maker and he did his best to stay out of the way,' he told the *Irish Sunday Mirror.* 'He ran the house with the efficiency of a military camp while my mother helped run the country. He wasn't a tactile man. I remember when my big sister Fiona was emigrating to Australia and I saw my mother crying in the hall at the bottom of the stairs.

'My father was hugging her, then he spotted me at the top of the stairs and pushed her away. He never showed his affections, whereas I'm the complete opposite – I'm like my mother because I'm always hugging people.

'I have very few memories of my father so I didn't really feel the loss. In many ways my mother made up for losing my father at such a young age. I was playing mental chess with her at the age of 11 and she introduced me to the theatre when I was 21.'

Brendan has admitted that the main influences on his life have been women, what with having a strong-willed mother, six sisters, and being the baby of the family. And when his father dad died, 'my mam filled both roles admirably. I had the individual attention of this genius and I was spoiled rotten.'

Brendan says his mother wasn't a mother in the 'mammy' sense, being so busy with politics and charity work: 'For instance, my sisters would remember a woman who they'd hear on the radio when they were kids decrying the fact that so many children were coming out of school illiterate,' he said on *Saturday Night with Miriam.* 'And she wouldn't be there to help them with *their* homework.

'My mother had a bachelors degree from university, so she obviously knew the importance of education, but none of her 11 children went past primary. Now we all did very well, it's just that she was a real contradiction. Her attitude always was "you'll be fine"... "just make the best of what you have" – and all 11 of us did fantastic.'

Brendan says he not only benefited from his mum's positive pushing and instilling in him a very, very positive attitude and being told he was the most wonderful thing in the world as a child, but also from the Moore Street market dealers and running errands for them and learning from them the value of a penny.

'For instance, if a small bag of potatoes cost 50 pence, and they were making 10 pence profit on that, before having a night out, they would actually sit down and think how many bags of potatoes that would cost them.'

When you consider that despite being widowed, his mother still found the time to raise her children, learn four languages, represent a constituency and become a chief whip and shadow minister for foreign affairs, then her son's ability to juggle several careers at once seems perfectly ordinary.

Agnes Browne's life, without Brendan's storytelling skill, does not seem nearly as interesting as the life of the author's mother, who died at age 71 in 1984. He would be still haunted by the death of his mother long after, and in 1997 he opened his heart on Irish television station RTE's *Would You Believe*, admitting: 'When my mother died, part of me died.

'I learned everything from my mother. She taught me that despite your social and educational background, despite poverty or deprivation, you can make something of yourself. When I was five years old she would say to me,

"Brendan, you can be anything you want to be." And I grew up believing that. I grew up with this unshakeable confidence. I grew up without fear.'

These days Brendan is not afraid to trumpet his own many accomplishments, with some justification. For this too, he credits his mother: 'She said that the one thing that you can give children is confidence and the responsibility to handle that confidence. She said that if you do something well, you should stand on the rooftop and say, "I did this!" And if something bad happens, you should do the same thing, and not try to appropriate blame.

'My mam loved and protected me from so many things, but in a way she loved me too much. I didn't really grow until she was gone. There's no breaking the bond.'

Talking to the *Scottish Sun*, he said: 'We had a very different home life and it wouldn't be unusual for my mother to be breast-feeding a wean on one arm while cradling the phone in the other and talking to Winston Churchill. With that kind of background and up-bringing, how could I not put a lot of my success down to her?'

Brendan told presenter Stephen Nolan on Radio Ulster's *The Stephen Nolan Show* that he wished his mother had been around to witness the success he has achieved with Mrs Brown: 'When my mother died I was a waiter, and she would loved to have seen all this, particularly the fact that I've written six novels, she was very much a reader and into books, and one of the great things she used to quote was people who were big enough to read at a place in New York called Rocky O'Sullivan's. It's a real literary hangout in New York, you don't ask to read in Rocky O'Sullivan's, you get invited to read and when you do it's the same as being asked to read at Harvard.

'I remember the night that I was asked to read in Rocky O'Sullivan's, and I remember the night before going down there, and my thoughts were, "God, she would have loved this".'

Nolan asked Brendan what he thought his mum would have said about crass language in the shows. 'She wouldn't think that at all,' said Brendan. 'First of all she would be very much in favour of the use of any available words in the English language. And she would also be of the opinion that the only four-letter words that are really offensive are things like "kill" or "rape" – these are much more offensive four-letter words than the f word.

'I know her opinion would be that it is side-splittingly funny, the reason would be that she is intelligent enough to not hear those words, she'd only hear the comedy.'

In the introduction to his book *The Young Wan*, Brendan said his mother told him 'Brendan, you can be anything you want to be; you, my son, can do anything.' He added, 'My mother left me one morning when I was 28. She took my son Danny, then just ten months old, for a mid-morning nap. He fell asleep, and so did she. I cannot tell you in just this one page of how wonderful a woman she was, but I promise that one day I will.'

After his mother died, 'everything I touched turned to muck', Brendan told Gay Byrne in his *The Meaning of Life* interview (RTE). 'I couldn't do a thing right,' he went on. 'And that's what I needed more than anything else in my life; I needed to fail – because there are no lessons in not failing. There are only lessons in failure.

'And I learned so much about myself, about my own character, my ability to go on, whether or not I would be an honourable person... I learned all that through failure. I'm very, very lucky that I have success now that I'm very pleased with and that I'm very, very comfortable with, but by God I feel I've earned it.'

CHAPTER 4

THE UNIVERSITY OF LIFE, LOVE & HAPPINESS

Brendan was only 12 when he left school, in many ways still very much a child but one that would have to learn to grow up fast. Today, he may be recognised as an acclaimed playwright, one of Ireland's most successful ever comedians – and he is a member of Mensa with an IQ of 153 to boot – but his early years were hard enough and a world away from the life he lives now. Yet, he would contend, the path he took gave him an education in life that has stood him in good stead for the career that was to come as a brilliant actor, comedian and writer.

'I'm dyslexic, and when you're dyslexic you feel that you're stupid,' he told Gay Byrne in a revealing interview for the RTE series *The Meaning of Life*.

'But I was also living with a genius, who didn't think I

31

was stupid, who had this theory to never confuse education with intelligence, they are two separate things. And she said you obviously can't learn the way the others are learning so we're going to have to find a different way for you to learn.

'But my mother was a contradiction. She thought the education system, it didn't teach you. It didn't prepare you for life. And she always felt we'd be alright, I don't know what it was, she always felt we were all people persons, we got on great with people. Because we had worked with me mam in the shelter, you get used to giving service without feeling servile.

'I love serving people. I love doing things for people and I never feel like a servant or a slave, I feel like I'm really contributing.'

Brendan's early working life was as a waiter – for all of 18 years – but other jobs included disco manager, milkman, painter-decorator and even a pirate radio disc jockey. He would later run his own bar and cabaret lounge before being forced to try the comedy circuit, but more of that later. Boxing legend Mohammad Ali famously once said, 'Even if I'd been a garbage man, I'd have been the world's greatest garbage man.' Brendan has that same winning mentality.

That same attitude he adopts to his professional and charity work these days, was shaped in his formative years, like when he worked as a cleaner in a factory. 'And a very good cleaner I was too,' he says. He was 13 going on 14 when he got his first 'proper' job as a waiter, a job that would allow him to develop his charm whilst also learning how to share in banter and acerbic put-downs. He wasn't content to be a person who simply served people food.

'I wanted to be the best waiter in the world,' he told the *Evening Times*. 'I loved to serve people and when they came into the hotel where I worked I wanted to make their day. I wanted to make sure that the experience they had was the best possible. Now, I know that the customer isn't always right, but he's always the customer. And I think if someone is paying for a service then they should be given the very best.

'And that's the attitude I've brought to my stage shows. I don't believe in short-changing people. So when audiences come to see a Mrs Brown show they get something different every night because I make sure myself, and the cast, put in a little something extra.'

It was only his natural curiosity – and inability to sit still – that took him from waiting tables to trying other career options. Aged 13, Brendan had a go at running a nightclub. He's also been a roadie for the comedian and singer Brendan Grace, a magazine publisher and an insurance salesman. And, when the business ideas bottomed out, he'd return to working as a waiter.

'Being a waiter was a profession back then, a very serious thing,' he told the *Sunday Times*. 'You had to learn it for four years. I was a commis waiter in the Skylon Hotel in 1969, the year it opened. Thanks to my mother's connections I was able to get a union card at just 12. I was 4ft tall and skinny as a bamboo. The head waiter, Teddy Gough, called all the waiters together and pointed at me saying, "Look at this. I ask the union for waiters and they send me a leprechaun."

'I loved him and he was one of my first mentors. My wages were 18s 6d, about one euro. Mind you, I made so much on tips I used to collect my wages every few weeks. It all went to me mammy.'

Brendan also worked as a waiter at the famous Gresham Hotel on Dublin's main thoroughfare, O'Connell Street, which would later feature in his first novel, *The Mammy*: 'It is Dublin's best hotel and I loved it.' In the hotel business he was nicknamed 'TC' – Top Cat. He also developed a love of cooking and had training as a chef.

But in an interview with the *Scottish Sun*, he confessed that growing up with a genius parent did have its drawbacks: 'By the time I was six I could be in one room and my mother in another and we could still play chess with no board and just from memory.

'But when I left school at 13 to train as a waiter I discovered that being ultra-smart did have a downside. I was training with dozens of other kids, but I couldn't seem to make friends with any of them.

'It was then I realised that I constantly corrected them and handed out so much advice that I sounded more like their dad than a pal. It dawned on me that I was a right boring bastard. I figured that to make friends and fit in I would have to bite my tongue and keep my head down. And that's exactly what I did for the next 25 years; that way I thought that people would like me.'

During his career as a waiter Brendan served drinks to legendary film stars Richard Burton and Elizabeth Taylor, as well as the King and Queen of Denmark. But it wasn't the case that while carrying out menial tasks he was dreaming of a career for himself in show business.

'No, I really wasn't,' he told US radio host Barbara

Bogaev. 'I was quite contented and I continue to be quite contented with my life,' he says. 'And I continue to be amazed at how things are going because every day I wake up and I'm sure today's the day they're going to find out I'm just a waiter and they're all going to want their money back. But hopefully, it won't happen for a while yet.

'No, you might notice a trend there that we've all ended up as waiters or chefs. And that's because when my mam did retire from politics, she had £46,000 Irish pounds (IR£) saved. At that time, you could buy a house in Ireland for £17,000.

'But instead of buying a house for the family, we moved into a municipal owned house and rented it. And she bought two large houses and knocked them into one and opened a refuge for battered women, battered wives. We all worked in the refuge. We all cooked. We made beds. We served breakfast for the women and kids. And we spent years, all our childhoods, working in this refuge. So with the result that we all ended up in the hotel business, it came very natural to us to have service without servility.'

With his mum very nearly becoming a bride of Christ as a nun, it's no surprise that religion would still have its place in his home. Brendan, again in conversation with Irish television host Gay Byrne for *The Meaning of Life*, said that he believes in God, but not 'organised religion':

Up 'til my dad died we said the rosary. Every night. My mother used to do this thing that the family that prays together stays together. But when I stopped going to mass there were no objections, I was about 13.

I said the purpose of me going to mass was to get

communion. I had started masturbating at that stage, and I wasn't going into a box to tell anybody that I was masturbating. So because I couldn't get a good confession, I couldn't be in a state of grace and I couldn't get communion, so the whole thing seemed pointless. So she [his mother] didn't say to me "stop or you'll go blind", she just said if that's what you feel, that's what you feel.

I never identified with Catholicism really, I don't know why. In my teens I started to read the Bible, would you believe. And I found it very interesting as a novel. One of the passages I always remembered was a thing that Jesus said: "The closer you are to religion, the further you are from God."

And I thought about that. And I'm not talking about Catholicism, I'm talking about organised religion in general. At that time I started to look at what I believed were money-making machines. How come in Finglas we are poor, but we've one of the biggest churches in the country? And we all paid for that, door-to-door.

And the Pope being infallible. All those things made me question organised religion, but I never ever lost my faith in God.'

He had to learn and grow up fast – he even had to get used to the fact that he'd end up bald from an early age: 'Hair loss didn't happen to me late in life. I remember going in to the barbers at 15 and him saying you're not going to have this too long. I'm used to being bald.'

And as he became a teenager, Brendan met his first love

– Doreen Dowdall – who nine years later would become his first wife. When he first clapped eyes on the Finglas girl he was smitten and later described her as 'the most beautiful thing I've ever seen in my life'.

Reminiscing to the *Irish Sunday Mirror* in 1998, he said: 'We were 13 years old and I will never forget the moment we met. I was running a disco for skinheads and this big gang came to it, about 80 of them. Then I saw her – she was wearing a black crombie coat and loafers and I fell head over heels in love. She was and she still is gorgeous.'

That night he took her out and told her he was going to marry her.

She replied: 'I wouldn't have anything to do with ya, ya sap.'

Four years later she changed her mind and Valentine's Day would always have a special place in his heart – he proposed to Doreen on 14 February 1972. 'I was only 17 and she was 18. Her dad had died that Christmas and we had just had a row. She was very down, so I said "Let's get engaged." So we went and got a ring.'

Five years later in 1977 they were married. Madly in love and with a barrowload of dreams for a life of happiness together, the devoted couple were keen to start a family as soon as possible.

CHAPTER 5

THE HARDEST LOSS TO BEAR

When Brendan's wife Doreen became pregnant with their first child the couple were beside themselves with excitement. The baby was due in 1979, just two years into their fledgling marriage, and the O'Carrolls were ready for the challenge of rearing children.

'White picket fence, swing in the garden, going to take him to the zoo, going to take him to all the football matches, I had everything planned,' says Brendan.

But their dream became a nightmare when, with only a month of the pregnancy remaining, it became clear that something was not right. It marked the lowest point in Brendan's life when his first-born child, a boy named Brendan after him, died only three days after his birth. To

38

make matters worse, the ordeal of a difficult birth and a 96-hour labour to deliver the gravely ill little baby almost robbed Brendan of his wife too.

He opened his heart on the RTE programme *Would You Believe* in 2000: 'We knew when she was in delivery that he was not going to be well, as Doreen went through such an awful time. He lived only a few days and Doreen was very ill. I always turned to my mother for solace, but this time she was speechless. I was sitting with her staring at the telly and she just grabbed my hand and said, "This will pass." Now I use those words all the time.'

His courageous, emotional and painful story of love, loss and suffering is a heartache that many will identify with and Brendan's honesty about his darkest day is admirable. And there is no doubt his frank and moving account of the death of his little boy will give comfort to others who have suffered a similar loss.

After the traumatic birth, Brendan's boy was left paralysed and blind. He was dying of brain damage and would not have long in this world. Yet Brendan could not bear to look at his newborn son at first. He sat rocking back in forth in a chair with his face buried in his hands angry at the cruel fate that had befallen him as much as the gruelling labour had almost killed his wife. He initially considered the child a 'monster' because of this, before finally relenting and summoning the strength to take a look at his child.

'The room was full of babies in little incubators in separate glass compartments,' he told the *Irish Sunday Mirror*, 'and of course when I looked at the baby nearest me, the tag on the little cot had my name on it – "Infant O'Carroll".

'I tried to look away, but I couldn't. I could see his little foot which was all twisted. I looked down at the baby Doreen and I had made out of love for each other and saw the most beautiful blue eyes I'd ever seen. In that one moment, my whole life changed. I fell in love with the little fella.'

Brendan Junior, a victim of spina bifida, died after a heart-breaking, three-day struggle to live. The tragedy left a hole in Brendan's life which has never been filled to this day, despite his phenomenal success. He may be a man who has brought laughter to households across the world, in Britain, Ireland, North America, Australasia and beyond, but days of guilt and pain are etched deep in his memory.

'The pregnancy had seemed normal until the last month when she ballooned from eight stone to 11 in four weeks,' Brendan told the *Irish Daily Mirror*. 'We asked the doctors if that was unusual but they didn't seem too concerned.

'But when Doreen went into labour there were major problems. It lasted for 96 hours and she had to have two epidurals which left her paralysed from the waist down for 10 days. I knew Doreen was dying in the labour and I wanted to rip the baby out myself and hold my wife in my arms until she got better. I felt we'd created a killer. It was really touch and go and I was terrified for her. The doctors told me she was very ill but they were doing all they could to make her comfortable and keep her out of danger. But I was convinced she was going to die. By that stage I didn't give a damn about the baby because I was so frightened for Doreen.'

Distraught and desperate, Brendan paced the corridors of Dublin's National Maternity Hospital for four days praying for a miracle as his wife was fighting for her life.

There was little hope for his severely disabled baby. Blinded and brain damaged by treatment during and shortly after his traumatic birth, little Brendan was given just hours to live. Brendan, who was working as a gas salesman at the time, said: 'Doreen was exhausted. She had gone through hours of labour and fell into a really deep sleep that I thought she would never wake from.'

And when doctors broke the news that even if the child miraculously survived it would definitely never walk, the couple simply discussed how they would afford a wheelchair.

'No problem that Brendan had was too great. Doreen had bonded with him the moment she held him in her arms. And after struggling not to love him, I was totally hooked. At 22, I was the proudest dad on earth.'

But sadly little Brendan's condition deteriorated rapidly over the next two days. When they were told he had died, Brendan said he and Doreen held each other and cried. 'We cried for baby Brendan and for ourselves.'

'He lived three days, but he still lives, he's still living now,' Brendan told Australian TV Channel Seven's current affairs programme *Sunday Night*. 'You never lose that sense of loss. You never lose that sense of, I've three wonderful kids and you look at them and think, "I wonder what he would have been like at that age."

'To think you're going to go through your life without things happening to you or things not going according to plan would be a ridiculous thought. That hasn't happened to anybody. Everybody fails, everybody makes a mistake.'

Brendan found some crumb of comfort in prayer, he told Gay Byrne on *The Meaning of Life*: 'I pray at all times.

Turmoil, celebration, every time I've asked for help or peace. After my son died I got very, very down, very disillusioned with life because I was very young and I had everything prepared in my mind.

'And this happened and my plans all went out the window. And I just couldn't find peace in myself, I couldn't be peaceful. And I asked for peace and it came, but with people, with friends. It nearly killed me. It was absolutely devastating. It tore my heart out. It still does.

'I didn't blame God at that stage, I didn't think it was his fault. I did later on, at different other things. What did I do? Was I so bad that I deserved this? Brendan had spina bifida and in order for him to be born, they had to operate on him while he was still in the womb. They had to remove some fluid from the brain. And every time they removed fluid, it would damage him. So when he was born, he was blind at that stage. Then the next he was paralysed, and it was a gradual disintegration. And I remember kneeling and begging God to take him.'

To this day though, Brendan told Gay Byrne, he believes there is spirituality surrounding his life. He said that Bishop Brendan Comiskey once told him, 'Brendan, you're one of God's people. You don't just talk the message of God, you live the message of God.'

'And that's what I'd hope, I hope that there's a karma, that I speak to everybody when I'm speaking in my car, that God is everybody, and when you're saying "please, please help me", I'm not asking for spiritual intervention, I'm hoping that you come around the corner and say "Are you under pressure?"

'I don't think there's a religiosity about me; I'd feel like a fake. One of the things that happens to me now if I go to mass, even for friends' weddings or Holy Communions, I do feel a bit hypocritical, because I'm standing there going, "I don't really believe this is the place of God."

'My home is the place of God, my heart is the place of God, my car... I do more talking to God in my car than I've ever done in a church. Ever.'

In the days that followed his son's death, Brendan dug deep to try to find the strength to keep both his and his wife's spirits up, but Doreen slipped into a deep depression and no one could get through to her.

'When she left hospital,' he told the *Irish Mirror*, 'Doreen went to bed and didn't get up for six weeks. She couldn't eat, she couldn't sleep and she cried herself hoarse. I kept trying to encourage her to get up and get on with it. Friends, family and even the doctors told me the best thing for Doreen would be to get pregnant again as soon as possible, but she couldn't even talk to me, let alone make love to me.'

But one night Doreen had a bizarre dream or vision which pulled her back to the real world.

Brendan says, 'Doreen had a vision of Our Lady who was holding a baby in a blanket one minute and a beautiful bunch of roses, the next. She told her that Brendan was safe and in the right place looking over her.

'Doreen felt so comforted by the dream. She said, "Brendan, everything's going to be alright. It's all going to be alright." I told her I knew it was and that I had been telling her that for the past six weeks.

'Then she climbed out of bed, cleaned the house, made

the dinner and got on with it. I couldn't believe it. For six weeks I hadn't been able to get through to her. She was depressed about losing Brendan and possibly suffering post-natal depression on top of that but the moment she got up, our lives started again.'

The drama and pain of losing Brendan Jr made Brendan Sr frantic with worry three years later when his wife was expecting again. But their daughter Fiona arrived, big, bouncy and healthy in 1980. 'I remember when the midwife rang in the middle of the night to tell me I had a baby daughter,' Brendan told RTE's *Would You Believe*.

'The first question I asked was, "What's wrong with her?" I rushed straight to the Coombe hospital and the first thing I saw was this amazing bundle of black hair – she had hair everywhere. She was absolutely gorgeous!'

Three years after the arrival of Fiona, who now plays Maria, the wife of Agnes' son Dermot in *Mrs Brown's Boys*, their son Danny was born. He would also come to star in *Mrs Brown's Boys* as loveable rogue Buster Brady. Brendan and Doreen would have one more child, Eric.

Fiona and Danny were 12 and 9, respectively, when their fourth child, Eric, was born in 1992. 'I had mixed feelings, I suppose,' Brendan said on *Would You Believe*, 'of discovering there would be a new baby, when the other two were heading towards their teens.

'We were starting to have more free time to ourselves, but really, I would have happily had 25 kids. I love them and I don't know what motivated me before them. I don't know why I got up in the morning before I had them.'

When the three children were growing up, Brendan and

Doreen made sure they knew all about the short sad life of their older brother, Brendan Junior: 'They understand what happened to Brendan and despite the fact that they never met him, they are aware how important he is in our lives.'

Brendan O'Carroll is a very proud dad and says that all his kids have had a profound influence on him, brought him joy and changed his life forever: 'Every single one of my kids brought something extra to my life. But I do feel lucky that, apart from Brendan, the rest of my kids are all fit and healthy.'

When he and his daughter Fiona were interviewed for the RTE programme *Would You Believe – Dads* in 2005, Brendan revealed that from the day that Fiona was born it forced him to work harder and he set out with the ambition to make as much money as possible so that he would be able to give her the best wedding possible when she was older.

Fiona recalled: 'All he ever wanted was to pay for his daughter's wedding and he has always said it will be a great wedding.' Brendan, said he had always tried to be a good father, adding, 'They are the reason you were born. I'd have nothing without them. I look at them and think – this is it.'

CHAPTER 6

A NEW CAREER IS ON THE MENU

Brendan had tried his hand at a string of jobs and had been a waiter through his teens and early adult life, but in 1990, in true showbiz saga style, his 'big break' arrived, and typically it came in the most unlikely fashion. His life changed when he took over the Finglas Castle bar and cabaret lounge in Dublin with an often-absent partner who turned out to have a serious drug problem.

'A bloke named Kevin that I had been working with told me about a choice pub that was for sale,' Brendan told the *Toronto Star*. 'We bought it together and Lord, did it prosper! The money was coming in hand over fist and I thought, "This is it, I'm safe for life!"'

But the working relationship with Kevin was fraught with constant problems concerning his drug habit which

46

meant Brendan had to keep dipping him in and out of rehab over the three years they worked in it together.

'We were holding on, but just,' recalled Brendan, 'and then my sister Fiona was getting married in Toronto. I had never taken a day off but I had to be there. I told Kevin I was going and he said "Brendan, this is the biggest vote of confidence anyone could give me. I'll do you proud."'

Two weeks later, Brendan returned to find desolation. 'Three days after I left, Kevin sold everything in the pub and fled with the money. I came back from Toronto and he was gone. And the tables were gone. And the chairs were gone. And the light fittings were gone. And all the beer was gone. And I left the pub and came back to a warehouse. I was IR£150,000 in debt. So I was desperate. For the first time in my life, I owed more than I owned. I tried to hate Kevin, but I couldn't. The poor bastard later died of AIDS.'

But forgiveness wouldn't pay the bills after going bust, so broke and desperate, Brendan turned to stand-up. He knew he could tell jokes in company and even to a crowd, having been encouraged a couple of times to the stage at the Finglas Castle by his friend Gerry Browne, a musician who'd also enjoy banter with his audience. Gerry would play in the pub with his folk group Tinker's Fancy and had asked Brendan once or twice to help out with a few gags to pad out his set.

Then he asked Gerry, a regular on the Dublin pub circuit, to get him a gig. There was no real pressure in cracking a few funnies in his own pub, but now he found himself, at the age of 35, standing on stage trying his hand at comedy to make a living.

'I didn't really have a plan that I was going to go into

comedy,' he told the *Scottish Sun*. 'And my mates had always said for years, "you should be on the stage". But you can't trust your mates.

'I was the youngest of 11 kids; I think you learn very quickly that if you can entertain the rest, if you can make the rest of them laugh, that you get very well looked after, you know. You might just get that last potato on the plate. I'd always told jokes at parties. And I knew at a party I could keep an audience, you know, entertained. But that's OK, because I'd be in the humour. But what if you're not in the humour? That's where the pro comes in, and I wasn't sure I could do it then.'

The nerves were jangling on the night of 12 October 1990. His stage debut would be at the rough and ready Rathmines Inn, an unforgiving audience if ever there would be one. As the 40 or so punters knocked back the booze, Brendan was squinting through the glare of the spotlight and the smoke-filled haze of the lounge room to gauge which gags went down well, and which didn't.

He admits he 'struggled' that first night but he came to realise that dirty jokes were going down a treat. That would be the way to go, he thought to himself.

As word spread of this outrageous comic, within six weeks there were 750 people at the venue. 'I just opened my mouth and it all came out, like verbal diarrhoea, but everyone seemed to think it was funny. There you go, it worked. When I tried it, it was just unbelievable. The first time I went on the stage I remember the feeling of "oh my god, it's so free, it's so freeing". And I knew in that moment it was my calling.'

That's when it all began. Fate had opened a door to a new

life for Brendan O'Carroll and he didn't think twice. He didn't just peek his head in to see what it was like, no, he barged through it. Word soon got round about this original and outrageous comedian and then there was standing-room only.

His in-yer-face brand of bawdy comedy was causing such a stir that the newspaper critics turned up to see what all the fuss was about. His stand-up act was described as being 'as blue as a frost-bitten penis' and Gerry Browne says it reached Roy 'Chubby' Brown levels of crudeness.

Brendan was calling himself 'The Baldy Fella', a nod to his hair loss but also a lewd reference to the penis, and was performing a miracle by packing out the Rathmines Inn on Tuesday nights with his bluer than blue take on Cilla Black's hit TV show *Blind Date*.

Talking to Australian TV Channel Seven's current affairs programme *Sunday Night*, Brendan gave an insight into his version of *Blind Date*:

'I had three girls on the stage: "What's the first thing you look for in a man?" There were two really posh girls and a really Dublin girl at the end.

'So the first posh girl said, "Eyes, I like eyes, a man with strong eyes."

'So I go, "Strong eyes?" and think, "Please God, make me funny."

'I go to the second girl and she said, "I like a man with a good swagger, who carries himself well."

'But the third girl said – and here's where you can get your bleeper in – "I don't care as long as he has a big cock."

'And the place fell apart laughing, and what I twigged in that moment was, that girl did nothing other than be herself. I'd spent years being somebody else, depending on what I was doing, why don't I just try at being myself?'

A journalist, Damian Corless, who went to see his act said that 'not only was the venue stuffed to the rafters, but the show was as foul as a backed-up sewer'. He added, 'Both the performer and his audience seemed fired up with an obscenity bloodlust. No comment was too gross, no target too soft.'

The crowd clearly loved it, but the journalist found the content hard to stomach. His *Irish Independent* review said: 'The Baldy Fella wasn't funny in any conventional sense. He wasn't funny in any unconventional sense either. He was just racist, sexist, homophobic and very, very dumb.'

Brendan's response was out of the ordinary. He had taken it to heart, having never had a review before. He wrote the critic a letter saying, 'I read what you wrote and you're right. I will change my ways.' And Brendan did eventually change his ways, honing his act so that it still had bite and plenty of bad language, but without the hardcore vulgarity.

'I did the stand-up act because I had to eat and so did my family,' he says. 'I literally didn't have a penny, and that's the truth. From there it just began to snowball and I began to make a living out of it.'

But it was tough at the beginning. Once he performed to just four people. 'I suppose other blokes would have given the punters their money back and gone home, but I stuck with it and had a great night,' he told the *Evening Times*. 'And you know, one person there recommended me to a bloke who booked me for a lot of money.

'The first time, I was paid IR£75. Two weeks later, I was given IR£750. It took off that quickly. The comedy club circuit was very cliquish, so I started performing where there weren't comedy clubs. I got together a band, a van, lights and even a portable stage. It was a travelling circus. We performed at pubs all over Ireland.'

Losing his own pub had turned out to be the making of him.

Brendan's partner in crime on the comedy circuit, yet again like in his childhood, would be Gerry Browne. After giving him his first chance to try stand-up, Gerry noticed that he was soon getting the hang of it and saw an opportunity for them to join forces with *The Outrageous Comedy Show* – a mix of gags, live music and comedy sketches.

'We started doing gigs around the country and I wasn't sure whether Ireland was ready for our act,' he told the *Irish Sunday Mirror*. 'We did get some adverse reaction – some people called us "dirty Dublin bastards". But mostly the audience loved the show. We offered them a different form of entertainment and they always came back for more.

'The best way to describe the act was that it was rude, crude and lewd – but the audience loved it. We released a single which reached No 8 in the Irish charts before we got our big break. It was called "Merry Christmas to the Irish Everywhere".'

More recently, there have been days when Gerry has struggled for cash, even being forced to go on the dole at one stage, but he maintains he was not bitter about playing second fiddle as Brendan steadily became a big-name celebrity as his career mushroomed with novels, plays and more.

'Some people are surprised when I say that I don't feel bitter about the way my career has developed so far,' he says. 'We deliberately set out to market Brendan as the main act because I thought then and still do that the man is a genius – he's absolutely incredible.'

CHAPTER 7

THE BIG C STRIKES

Brendan and Doreen thought they had already had their fair share of heartache when they lost their first-born child. On top of that, they were struggling under the strain of money worries while Brendan fought to clear debts after his pub business collapsed.

There was much more than a glimmer of hope though as his comedy career was starting to take off and finally it seemed their luck was changing. But all the while, however, Brendan's on-stage laughter was hiding his tears over a secret heartache his growing legion of fans knew nothing about.

He had been left stunned by the bombshell news of another threat to his precious wife's life – she had been diagnosed with breast cancer. And worse still, she was pregnant for the fourth time, and doctors told them she would lose the child as a result of chemotherapy.

Brendan had no doubts that the terrible turn of events went hand in glove, blaming the stress of their financial problems for making his wife ill.

'The pressure on the family was terrible,' he told the *Irish Sun*. 'I'm convinced that was responsible for Doreen developing breast cancer. I was out all the time but she had to live with this every day. She used to dread seeing the postman in case it was another bill.'

He himself struggled to cope but rather than his wife see him buckling under the pressure he would go away to sob quietly to himself.

'Some nights I would get into the car, drive to a quiet place and cry my eyes out,' he remembers.

Doreen was diagnosed with breast cancer in September 1991 when she was pregnant with their son Eric.

'The lump on her breast was only the size of the knuckle on my first finger when she first discovered it,' says Brendan. 'But within three weeks it was as big as my fist.' His now-famous self-belief and positivity momentarily deserted him as they stared death in the face and he was initially not much help.

'I thought she was going to die,' he admitted to the *Irish Mirror*. 'I chain-smoked and we sat around talking after they broke the news. Doreen sobbed "I'm going to die", and I said "I know". I was no good at that stage.' The couple stayed up for nights on end, talking about the good times in the past and what the future might hold for them.

Brendan had taken a Positive Mental Attitude (PMA) course 12 years earlier which would later become the basis for his first venture as a playwright. And it was that course that also helped during those dark hours when death cast a shadow over them. 'Fortunately, PMA is infectious,' says Brendan. 'We soon decided anything other than Doreen dying would be a victory. Dying was the worst possible scenario imaginable.'

Doreen had a breast removed, but mercifully the couple were given hope when they were told that she had a slim chance of holding on to the baby. Eric was born 15 weeks premature and weighed just three pounds.

Brendan was able to find an escape in his regular two-hour stage shows: 'I was in another world with no worries for the length of the show. The old saying "Dr Theatre will cure you" is really true. And the boys in the band helped me laugh. Laughter gives you the strength to cope.'

On the night the baby was born, Brendan went on stage and dedicated a song to Doreen and Eric, telling the crowd his new son only weighed three pounds.

Doreen and the baby spent four months in hospital while she received chemotherapy. By the end of 1993 she had finished the course and was finally given the all clear.

Brendan believes the baby saved his wife's life, because the cancer would not have accelerated so quickly had she not been pregnant when they first noticed the tiny lump and thought about taking action.

He would later raise awareness of breast cancer by weaving it into the plot of his first novel, *The Mammy*, in which Agnes Browne's best friend Marion Monks would die from the disease, and again in his hit TV series *Mrs Brown's Boys*.

To this day he still has nothing but praise and admiration

for his wife: 'She's very strong and inspirational.' He added at the time. 'At the moment she's counselling some friends in the same position as we were. She's a pillar of strength and I love her.'

CHAPTER 8

MOTHER OF INVENTION – THE BIRTH OF AGNES

Agnes Brown, the much-loved, foul-mouthed matriarch who is the hero of the hit television series *Mrs Brown's Boys*, began as a bluff. And she started life as Agnes Browne, with an 'e'.

It was 1992 and Brendan's comedy career was taking off as a stand-up when he was invited on to Gareth O'Callaghan's RTE Radio 2fm show. As they chatted afterward, Gareth explained that he was looking for 'something quirky' for his show and Brendan, quick to spot an opportunity, blurted out that he had been working on a comedy soap opera – *Mrs Browne's Boys*.

It was a defining moment in his career, a typical O'Carroll gamble which could have just as easily turned into nothing but, as Brendan has always found during his career, fortune favours the brave. 'He was crying with laughter by the end of the show,' Brendan told the *Newcastle Journal*. 'And the presenter came over to where me and my agent were sitting and started talking.

'He told me he was looking for something quirky for the afternoon slot and – much to the surprise of my agent – I said I was writing a five-minute comedy soap opera. It was completely off the top of my head. When he asked what it was about, my agent, who knew I hadn't written anything, got a very worried look on his face.

'But I just started making it up as I went along and said it was about a Dublin housewife with six grown-up children that she still treats like young kids. I called it *Mrs Browne's Boys*.'

Talking to Australian TV Channel Seven's current affairs programme *Sunday Night* in 2013, Brendan revealed how the show's title came about: 'The day we had done it [the radio interview] was the anniversary of the first test tube baby, who was Louise Brown. I was reading it that morning and when he [the presenter] said "What's it called?" I said, "Mrs Browne's Boys".'

(The different spelling of Brown came courtesy of his stage partner Gerry Browne. The pair often worked on material in the kitchen of Annie Browne, Gerry's mother. She may also have inspired the name, but Brendan has always said that the character of Agnes herself was a combination of many influences, from his mother who he adored so much, to the Moore Street market traders he looked up to as a boy. Brendan would reprise the star of *Mrs Browne's Boys* the radio show to develop *Mrs Brown's*

Boys the stage show and later the TV series, shedding the 'e' as if to mark a new chapter in his life.)

'The radio presenter said "I'd love to see the first three episodes" and my agent said "So would I." So I went home and rattled out the first 10 episodes. It was completely made up on the spot. I wrote the shows and a few weeks later they used them.'

In an interview with Mark Lawson on *BBC Radio 4* on 25 April 2012, Brendan would elaborate more on this twist of fate – and the lie – that led the conception of Agnes:

I'm a waiter by trade and one of the things you have to learn as a waiter is how to make up a lie very quickly. When somebody says, 'Why is there no beef?', rather than say 'the chef actually hung himself out the back and we're having a bit of a crisis in the kitchen', it's easier to say 'actually we had a very very big order from somebody very important in Dublin Castle, otherwise we'd have it for you'.

So I'm good at making up lies. And that's basically how it happened. And Rory [Cowan] who plays Rory in the series, was my press agent at the time, and Rory joined us and I said just off the top of my head, 'I'm writing something, it's a five-minute radio piece. It's a soap, five minutes a day, five days a week.'

And the guy was on it like a rash: 'Really are you?' And my agent went – 'Are you?' So he said he'd love to hear it so that weekend I went and I wrote 10 episodes which would have been two weeks, 10 five-minute episodes.

I got anybody I could to record it so if you look at

the cast that are there now, the ones who are still there from the radio series, Grandad for instance, he was my window cleaner. But I needed a voice so I brought him in to do a voice on the radio.

Rory who plays Rory, he was always there and has that voice without having to put it on, I won't go there, so I used any voices I could, sent it to him and he came back and said 'No, they won't run it because she says bum and it's going on at half four in the afternoon so they won't run it.'

So I thought that will be it, and literally two months later he called me and said 'My producer's going on holiday and I've been told to produce the show myself for two weeks, so I'm going to run it.'

And he ran it. And by the fourth episode the head of the station asked me to come in and see him, he said he wanted to commission the show but he had no money. He said 'we don't have a drama budget' so he offered to pay me in T-shirts, and I took it. So we got paid 150 T-shirts a week, which we sold at the gigs. It was supposed to run for two weeks and it ran for two-and-a-half years.

Brendan has said that initially his blag, or boast, to the radio presenter centred on him writing *Mrs Browne's Boys* – he hadn't intended to star in it as the central character.

'I'd actually hired an actress for the voice of Mrs Browne,' he told the *Northern Echo*. 'But she dropped out the day we were due to record, so I had to step in myself. I literally fell into it by accident because the actress who was due to play Mrs Browne on the radio series pulled out because she had a kidney infection.

'I found out years later that Willy Russell, who wrote *Shirley Valentine*, had to play the role himself for six weeks because Pauline Collins also got a kidney infection. Mind you, he's talented and I'm just getting away with it.'

Brendan had then planned to use an actress to re-record the dialogue later. But when one of the recording crew asked later where he found the actress playing Mrs Browne, as she was very good, Brendan realised he could do it himself 'and it was another wage I didn't have to pay'.

He adds, 'I really thought it would only take off in Dublin, I didn't even think it would take off outside of Dublin in the rest of the country. Over the time that followed, we had so many people guesting on the show, like Gabriel Byrne, but that's where it all started and I can still hardly believe how far it has come.'

Initially, Brendan wanted to switch back to the original cast, but the editing staff persuaded him to stay on. 'So the whole thing is a big accident,' he jokes.

His undoubted talent for diversification would later become evident in the multitude of ways in which he would continue to exploit his most enduring creation, Agnes Browne. 'That five-minute piece that I wrote for radio became four novels, a film starring Anjelica Huston, a film now being made [in 2013] starring myself as Mrs Brown, five stage plays, a TV series and a radio series,' he says. 'All out of that one woman's story, which is astounding,' he told the *Northern Echo*.

Nothing, least of all death, has stood in the way of Agnes's success story. Even though Brendan killed off the character in the radio show and his third book, *The Granny*, she of course still very much lives on in his plays and TV series.

'She's now older than she was when she died in the books,' says Brendan. 'I can give her a son if it suits me and that son will never appear again. Listen, it's not Shakespeare. It's just comedy. Whatever I can write, or rob, I can fit into Mrs Brown.'

So who is actually is Mrs Browne, with or without an 'e'? Is she Brendan's mother? These are the two questions Brendan gets asked the most, and his answers have varied over time.

'Mrs Browne is based on my mother-in-law,' he said in one explanation in a very early interview with the *Irish Times*, 'and she's exactly like Mrs Browne in that the entire world revolves around her family. Her family is her world – regardless of their shortcomings, she loves them all beyond reason.'

Though largely a music hall archetype, in truth she would be an amalgamation of a host of different women Brendan encountered in his youth and mainly, says Brendan, Dublin's rough and ready market traders.

Brendan also drew on the days when he earned pocket money by running errands for the dealers in Moore Street. His memories of the women who ran the market's fruit and veg stalls with 'hearts of gold but hard as rocks' also helped to form the backbone for what became Agnes Browne.

'These women all had the same thing in common', he told the *Liverpool Daily Post*. 'Even if their lives were falling apart, they all believed their ship was just over the island. The wisdom is there – it's either black or its white, there is no grey.

'The extraordinary thing is that the stalls all sell the same things and the women are pretty rough and take no prisoners. There is no such thing as the suspension of language. They get married at 19 and become 40 immediately, have kids and raise a family. Then, when they *are* 40 and the kids are doing their own things, they become 16.

'You get these women of 40, 50 and 60 talking like teenagers and coupled with colloquial language you are going to get something quite extraordinary – like Mrs Browne. One of the questions I get asked most of all is, Mrs Browne, is she your mother? I used to say "absolutely not" because my mother is a completely different type of character and Mrs Browne is a collage of all those women I know on Moore Street.

'And they were very strong women and they had a great optimism, and that's what I saw in Moore Street, and that's what I felt in Moore Street, and that's what I tried to put into Mrs Browne.

'Moore Street is where Molly Malone originally plied her trade. The market stalls are run by tough, hard women, and they have a great turn of phrase, really quick wit. They're as tough as nails but with hearts of gold.

'And they've got a great optimism about them, even when their lives are falling apart they still believe their dreams are going to come true, that their ship is just off the horizon. I found them very inspirational, so I used to run errands for these old dears, helping to pack, tidying up boxes, sometimes minding the stall while they went for a quick lunch. And just all those voices merging together became Mrs Browne.'

The battle-scarred matriarch with the sharp but foul-mouthed tongue while not based on his mother, as he has at times maintained, instead reflected his childhood when women were second class citizens, he says.

'This submissiveness is passed from generation to generation. Agnes is one of the links that broke the chain,' he says. He would relent in later interviews, though, and admit that he could see similar qualities in Agnes to that of his mum.

'The more I've done book readings around the world and the more I've spoken about Mrs Brown, the more I'm starting to see, you know I think Mrs Brown is my mam – without the education. But she is my mam – or there's a possibility, that Mrs Brown was the mother that I wanted to have.'

In 2011, he told interviewer Georgina Wahed from *thefancarpet.com* more about the influences on Agnes: 'When my mum retired from politics and stepped back a bit and stayed at home to look after me, she'd made a few bob, she'd done okay, and we thought we'd be okay, but she bought two homes on the North Circular Road and she knocked them into one and she opened a shelter for battered wives and homeless kids in which we all had to volunteer, whether we wanted to our not.

'I thought she was completely the opposite, immediately I would have rejected that Mrs Brown was anything to do with my mum, but as I get on I start to see lots of similarities. The difference is, Agnes left school when she was 10. My mother had a Bachelor's degree from Galway University. Education is the only difference but they're exactly the same. My mother was exactly the same with her kids.'

So the creation of Agnes would be influenced by various women Brendan encountered throughout his life – his first mother-in-law, his friend Gerry Browne's mother, the market traders of Moore Street, and a hint of his mum thrown in for good measure. Above all, she was to represent a typical Irish mammy.

In an interview with the *Newcastle Evening Chronicle*, Brendan said that he considered himself very lucky that he lived the Mrs Browne life: 'Mrs Browne's environment was my environment growing up. So it's not a question of me trying to make up and wonder what these people do,' he says. 'Every family around us was like us. We were all poor but we didn't know we were poor because we were all the same.

'In all the Mrs Brown plays, when the tragedy is at its worst, the comedy is at its highest. That's the way we cope. You won't have more fun than at an Irish funeral. We coped that way with the laughter. So it came very naturally.'

So we've learnt that Mrs Browne/Brown is based on an amalgamation of women – but when it came to actually playing her, one other big influence was actually a man.

'My main inspiration was an old Irish actor named Cecil Sheridan,' he told the *Liverpool Daily Post*. 'He was one of the stalwarts of the old Theatre Royal in Dublin, and he used to play this larger-than-life Dublin woman who commented on life. I can't recall the character's name, I am not sure she ever had one.'

Brendan first met him working as a waiter in a hotel where Sheridan was doing a cabaret turn. He was surprised to discover he had a terrible stutter, particularly as on stage there was no sign of one. 'Doctor Theatre, he cures everything,' the old actor explained.

CHAPTER 9

BETTER LATE LATE THAN NEVER

Brendan's radio play *Mrs Browne's Boys* became a rip-roaring instant success. 'I couldn't believe that it took off in such a huge way,' Brendan told the *Allentown Morning Call*. 'Prisoners asked to be put in their cells early, cows were put in early, and factories changed their tea breaks just so people could listen to it.

'The show ran five minutes a day, five days a week for more than two years. To my surprise it captured the entire nation. It was on at half past four every day, and at half past four you could not get a taxicab in Dublin.

'At half past four the prisoners in Wheatfield Prison demanded to be locked up so they could hear this on the radio. Factories went on their tea breaks. She just captured the entire country.'

Brendan managed to churn out some 370 episodes of the show as fans became hooked. In turn it meant that Brendan was becoming in even more demand as a stand-up comedian at the same time, with his blue, no-holds-barred pub shows becoming a hit across Ireland. He was so successful – and hard-working – that he was able to pay back his failed pub-business debts in four years by working non-stop.

By this stage Brendan had paired up with his old childhood friend Gerry Browne and they produced *The Outrageous Comedy Show* which was a mix of gags, live music and comedy sketches like the filthy version of *Blind Date*.

But in the early days they still had to get up at dawn for Gerry's milk round as well. Gerry had lent him IR£10,000 to make initial repayments on his debts and the two subsequently teamed up as a cabaret double act to recoup the money. They would continue to share all profits and investments on a 50/50 basis.

The radio success brought Brendan to the attention of television. And the turning point in the comedian's career came about in February 1993, when he got his big break on the biggest TV show in Ireland, *The Late Late Show*, Ireland's longest running chat show.

Its presenter Gay Byrne is a national institution to the people of Ireland. The UK had Michael Parkinson and the States had Johnny Carson, but 'Gaybo' is more than a chat show host. Now retired, he was a window on the world, he was often controversial by debating hot topics, he brought international culture to Irish screens while promoting its own – and he helped to launch hundreds of careers.

And when, in February 1993, he introduced former waiter Brendan O'Carroll on to *The Late Late Show*, the 35-minute interview that followed propelled Brendan into the pantheon of Irish greats. Gaybo would do for him what Parky did for Billy Connolly.

While Gay would be the platform to propel Brendan to bigger things, the responsibility lay with Brendan to once again seize an opportunity. People knew of the *Mrs Browne's Boys* radio show but knew nothing of Brendan himself and he realised he had to win over Ireland's top broadcaster before he could win over the public.

He knew this was it. It was make or break time, it could be the first and last time he would get a chance like this. So Brendan knew he had to do something different; maybe something outrageous. He had to think of something that would make the most of this opportunity. And so he did. As he walked on the show, he broke convention by stopping a few feet short of his host, forcing Gaybo to get out of his seat and walk towards him.

'I was booked for a nine-minute interview on the strength of the radio show,' he told the *Irish Sunday Mirror*. 'People knew the series but not me. Thankfully the other guests weren't too hot that night. I thought I could really sparkle that night but I had never met Gay, I didn't know how far I could go. I was told to walk on and pause and then walk down to Gay.

'He said, "Welcome Brendan O'Carroll." I walked out and stopped where I had been told to pause and stood there – I wouldn't move.

'Gay said "good man, good man" and the audience kept clapping. I still didn't move. He then came out to get me.

He held my hand and tried to pull me to the chairs. I stood there and Gay had to get up to shake me hand. He tried to pull me down and as he did I pulled him back and said, "Howareya Gay? How's your willy?" He said, "Ahew"… and then a big smile broke on his face. Straight away I knew I was in. This happened off-mike so the TV audience didn't hear it. But I knew my gamble of doing things differently had worked.'

Veteran entertainer Gay Byrne wasn't fazed by Brendan, in fact he appeared to encourage him.

'Byrne said, "You are a terrible bold man – you're no altar boy are you?" I said, "No I'm not," then I told story after story and 10 minutes later he's on the floor laughing.

'The interview was due to be nine minutes long. I kept going and it turned out to be the longest interview with a comedian *The Late Late Show* had ever done and 35 minutes later he was wiping the tears from his eyes.

'I was an instant success. The next day everybody in the country knew my name – it was an amazing transformation and I will never forget the man who gave me the leg up. After that my career went through the roof. They wanted me everywhere.'

He and Gerry had been catapulted to fame and the money started rolling in. But not only was he a household name, he could now command top fees.

The *Late Late Show* appearance transformed him from a hit on the Dublin pub circuit into a nationwide box-office draw – he was so successful afterwards that in 1993 he played 317 consecutive dates.

The Godfather of Soul, James Brown, revelled in being

called the 'hardest-working man in show business', but Brendan O'Carroll would give him a run for his money. Within four years Brendan did more than 1,000 stand-up shows in Ireland, Britain and America. Brendan and Gerry were raking it in, so much so that the pair of them bought expensive new family homes in Ashbourne, Co Meath.

However, he bristles at the implication that Gay Byrne 'made' him a star. 'I made myself a fucking star,' he has said. 'Who else was on the *Late Late* that night? I made me.'

But years later, in another TV interview with Gay himself, Brendan said to him, 'You get great pleasure out of opening the door for people, and you did open the door for me that night, but I hope I kicked it in, I hope I kicked it through.'

After his expletive-laden debut on *The Late Late*, Brendan O'Carroll became a household name as he peddled his lewd brand of Dublin wit around the country and in further TV appearances. He would appear on the nation's favourite TV show a total of 24 times between 1992 and Byrne's retirement in 1999 and has been a regular fixture with the subsequent hosts since.

His live work rate was phenomenal, and spin-offs from the tours included flogging DVDs of his X-rated gigs. His first video, *Live at the Tivoli*, went straight to No 1, even managing to knock U2 out of the top slot.

He then made five other videos which also held No 1 slots, with sell-out tours of Ireland and the UK before Brendan, Gerry and their crew headed for North America and Australia.

They were laughing, literally, all the way to the bank.

CHAPTER 10

FROM MAMMY TO GRANNY – THE AGNES BROWNE TRILOGY

B rendan O'Carroll has proven to be a prolific writer, from the *Mrs Brown's Boys* plays and TV series to his novels. But the seeds of this career as a writer were sown thanks to meeting the actor Gabriel Byrne – star of such movies as *The Usual Suspects* – in New York in 1994.

Thanks to his growing reputation in Ireland, Brendan bagged a gig on the RTE team which travelled to America to cover the fortunes of the Republic of Ireland football team at the World Cup.

Brendan's role was to provide entertaining 'colour' pieces, and the 'straight man' he was paired up with was Niall Quinn, who played for Manchester City at the time but had not made the Ireland squad for the tournament.

Niall said spending that time with Brendan helped him

get over the disappointment of not playing at the prestigious event. 'I got to spend five weeks with Brendan,' he says. 'You couldn't feel sorry for yourself. We had a laugh. It was enjoyable.'

Ireland's first game was in New York at the Giants Stadium where they would shock red-hot favourites Italy by beating them 1-0, thanks to a spectacular Ray Houghton goal. The day before, Brendan appeared at a five-hour party, 'Lark in Gaelic Park', at Broadway and 240th Street in the Bronx, and took Niall Quinn with him.

Billed as a warm-up celebration before the football matches, it also featured music by the Wolfe Tones and Bagatelle and appearances by the singer Frances Black and Olympic runner Eamonn Coghlan.

Brendan was no stranger to the city, he had visited the Big Apple with his and Gerry's *Outrageous Comedy Show*, a favourite with expats and New York's big Irish community. And it was on one of those flying visits a few months before the World Cup that Brendan thought he would look up an old friend, Gabriel Byrne.

And that innocent coffee meeting would prove to be another life-changing twist of fate.

Brendan says, 'Gabriel had been at one of the shows and met me for a coffee, he initially discussed writing a screenplay. He was talking, but I wasn't listening because I was too busy looking around hoping someone would see me with Gabriel Byrne!'

Gabriel encouraged him to write a screenplay and sent him a book by the screenwriter Syd Field which recommends writing a 20-page back story on each character. Brendan's back story on Agnes Browne evolved into something much larger. It became Brendan's first novel, *The Mammy*, published later that year by The O'Brien Press.

Writing a new introduction to the novel when it was reprinted in 2011, Brendan revealed how the next stage in the evolution of Agnes took came to be:

I was sitting in the lobby of a Hilton Hotel in Orlando, Florida, when this book was born; it was 1994 and the Republic of Ireland had qualified for the finals of the World Cup.

I'd just begun to make a name for myself in Ireland as a comic and Tim O'Connor, Head of Sport for RTE (Irish TV) had employed me to travel with the team on their adventure and do some colour pieces to camera for the audience at home.

However, my job was to do a three-minute piece every second day. Well, anybody who knows me will tell you that so little work would drive me insane. So to while away the time, I bought a legal pad and a pen and I began to write. But what to write? Some months earlier the magnificent actor Gabriel Byrne had sent me a book by Syd Field, entitled Screenplay. *This book is amazing and a must-read for any aspiring scriptwriter. It suggests that a scriptwriter should compose a 'back story' for the main character in their movie. So that's what I decided to do. But I didn't have a movie.*

What I did have was a five-minute comedy soap called Mrs Browne's Boys *that was running Monday to Friday on 2fm's Gareth O'Callaghan Show. 'What a great exercise,' I thought, 'a 20-page back story on Mrs Browne.'*

So I began. Well nearly. I couldn't decide where to start. I didn't want to go back to her childhood, as that would require research into the 'times'. So I decided to start on the day she became a widow.

I opened the pad and began; I expected the 20 pages to take me an hour or so. Two weeks later I was still writing. The 20 became 30, 40 and on and on. By the time I had finished, I had only covered the first nine months of her widowhood. Satisfied, I closed the pad and thought no more about it.

Later on that trip, during a phone call with my then manager Pat Egan, I mentioned the writing. Pat called me three days later and told me that he had spoken to Michael O'Brien, the publisher at The O'Brien Press, and they wanted the book.

I protested a little. 'He hasn't even read it yet!' I said, worried that it was crap. Pat replied, 'He doesn't care, if it's about Mrs Browne he wants it.'

The Mammy was released a few months later and was number one in the bestseller list in its first week. The five-minute radio series led to this book, which led to three more books, which led to me writing a movie – Agnes Browne, starring Anjelica Huston.

The Mammy became a bestseller in Ireland and was followed by *The Chisellers* (a Dublin slang term for children) and *The Granny*, in which Agnes is about the age that she was in the original soap opera.

The premise of the books would be the life of this widow

Agnes Browne, struggling to raise her seven children on her own after the death of her husband Redser on a lowly wage as a market dealer selling fruit and vegetables.

Brendan's stories would be mixed with heartache and joy, rich in Dublin humour and with triumph over adversity, and the characters from the radio series that were developed through the books would then form the basis of the future *Mrs Brown's Boys* plays and TV series.

Agnes's sons Mark, Dermot, Rory and Trevor and daughter Cathy from the trilogy would make it to the shows, as would Dermot's partner in crime Buster Brady. So too would Mark's wife Betty, Rory's boyfriend Dino and also Maria Nicholson, although in the books she marries Trevor, Brendan would change that to Dermot for *Mrs Brown's Boys*.

The books also enjoyed worldwide success, especially in North America where Brendan would travel on book signing tours. While there is both comedy and sorrow in the trilogy, it is grounded in an upbeat view of life. 'I'm a happy guy,' Brendan says. 'I like writing happy endings. I don't want to punish my readers with sorrow.'

They were so successful in fact that Brendan would later publish, in 2003, a prequel to the series called *The Young Wan*, an Irish phrase for a girl. 'I killed her off in the third instalment, but the Yanks went crazy, so I wrote a fourth: *The Young Wan* which was a prequel to all of it when Mrs Browne was a child.'

Americans likened Brendan's work to a cross between *Angela's Ashes* author Frank McCourt and Roddy Doyle of *The Commitments* fame. Never short of ideas, Brendan had plans for another novel called *Jesus of Dublin*, about the Second Coming occurring in Ireland's capital, but that one hasn't yet been published.

'I was never a writer,' he says. 'I never wrote anything for the comedy shows, I'd just get up on stage and start chatting to the audience. Then one day I started writing about all the women I knew in my life and the *The Mammy* was completed. It was followed by *The Chisellers* and *The Granny*.'

With young children at home, Brendan found he could only write at night-time when they were in bed and the house was at peace.

It's something he has done throughout his career – and still does – as he moved on to writing plays, sitcoms and screenplays. He'd sit puffing on his panatela cigars, writing relentlessly all through the night, often finishing as the sun reared its head and the kids were getting up for school.

In his waking hours he works tirelessly, but even while asleep his mind is whirring with new ideas. 'In fact, this is the first time I've admitted this, but I get most of the ideas for my books and plays from dreams,' he told the *Irish Sunday Mirror*. 'One night I had a dream which turned out to the main plot for a new book, *The Bingo Ball Gang*. I woke up and started writing and I had the first 22 pages of the book completed before I knew it. So if I can do it, anybody can.'

'None of us realises how extraordinary our own lives are,' he told the *Allentown Morning Call*. 'We all face trials and tribulations. We all have extraordinary characters in our lives – the eccentric aunt or the mad uncle. Agnes Browne has a normal life, but doesn't realise how special it is. She is a woman on a voyage of discovery.

She does not need a man, which means that she would appreciate a man more.'

The Mammy spent 18 weeks on the *Irish Times* bestseller list before it went to the States and beyond on its global journey. It has outsold James Joyce's *Ulysses* in Ireland.

By the end of 1994, Brendan was working hard on many fronts – his sell-out stand-up shows, spin-off videos, and now bestselling novels. On top of this, he had TV work and plays in the pipeline. His diversification to become an author filled him with real pride though. He felt he had earned some respect and proved to his critics that there was more to him than filthy jokes.

On another promotional tour of the States in 2000, he told *National Public Radio* host Jacki Lydon how much he loves entertaining and telling stories, and sees himself as a traditional Irish storyteller no matter the entertainment vehicle.

'We have an Irish phrase which I know you're aware of, Jacki, called shanachie [seanchaí in Irish] and the shanachie's tradition is that, because of the banning by the English in the 1700s of us educating children, the shanachie's job was to go from village to village to relate the history in stories of that village or of that time so that the children could carry on the tradition or the history or a sense of history.

'And, of course, the shanachies became blatant liars. You know, all of a sudden, Cu Chulainn was 14-foot tall... and he could run through a forest, pulling thorns out of his feet with his teeth while he was running. But these made him magical and made him even easier for the children to remember, so they had a technique.

'Well, I would like to be remembered as a shanachie in some way, and in every way I possibly can, telling the story, whether it be radio, screenplay, movie, TV. It doesn't matter to me as long as I get to tell the story. It'd be nice to think that, 'cause I believe in magic.'

His books would prove to have such a worldwide appeal they would be translated into 17 different languages and by April 2000, within little over a year of their release in the States, the first two parts of the trilogy had sold nearly 175,000 copies and the star was asked to tour the US to promote the final part – *The Granny*.

The *New York Times* hailed *The Mammy* as 'heart-warming', knocked *The Chissellers* as 'schmaltz' and praised *The Granny* for its 'delicious dessert of an ending'. Throughout his career Brendan would divide critics, but the facts would speak for themselves anyway – the public couldn't get enough of him.

And Brendan couldn't care less what his detractors say, as long as he has bums on seats and books flying off the shelves.

CHAPTER 11

BRENDAN'S CAREER GETS ON COURSE

PMA stands for Positive Mental Attitude, something that Brendan O'Carroll vehemently believes in, knows all about, and has himself never lacked.

It is a system of self-belief which deems that anything can be achieved by those who convince themselves they can achieve it, and it formed the background to his first foray into theatre in 1995 with *The Course*. The play was about a group of no-hopers who sign on for a training session of PMA run by Joe Daly, played by Brendan. He gives courses to a 'motley group of losers' and he gets a good bonus for every person who passes the exams to get a job selling insurance.

No one fails, so that Joe pockets the cash and everything is going well until he gets rumbled and his American boss arrives and threatens to close down the course – unless everyone passes the exam. The oddball cast of characters, which includes a prostitute, a golf widow, an alcoholic and a resting actor, rise to the challenge, with unexpected and hilarious results.

'In Ireland in 1995, I'd become the new hot thing,' Brendan told the *Newcastle Evening Chronicle*, 'but everybody knows stand-up comedy only has a certain life, no matter how funny you think you are. I wanted to look at doing different things. I told a reporter I wanted to write a play for the Dublin Theatre Festival.

'I was aware that a Dublin writer hadn't been premiered at the Festival in over 80 years so I thought I'd have a go. Lo and behold, a month later I get a letter from the festival welcoming me and saying they were looking forward to seeing my play.'

The move was the first of many heart-stopping gambles with money that Brendan would make in his new career; he would let nothing stand in the way of becoming a success. He raised the finance himself and hired his own theatre. He had never written a play before nor ever produced one, but that didn't stop him. So off he went and hired a theatre, staging a co-production with Tivoli Theatre boss Tony Byrne.

And then the problems began. 'About four months later, Tony got a call from the Theatre Festival people saying that they needed my play for another production, and they asked would he swap my play over with another, smaller theatre,' he told the *Evening Times*.

'He asked me and I said "No". I needed the larger theatre to make sure of getting my money back, given the size of the cast and the costs of renting the theatre and production costs.'

The theatre owner was petrified that this would upset the Theatre Festival people, and begged Brendan to cancel his booking and go elsewhere. But when Brendan again said 'no' the Festival organisers were determined to try and scupper his plans.

'A couple of weeks later I read in the paper that the Theatre Festival Committee had rejected my play. Now, this was quite an amazing thing, because the Festival people had never even read my play. In fact, I hadn't read it – because I hadn't written it.'

Clearly, if Brendan wasn't going to back down, the big boys were going to try and bury him. 'It was ironic, but the Positive Mental Attitude really kicked in. It gave me the determination I needed to go on.'

However, then he came up against a problem that would have terrified most: 'Tony Byrne, the theatre boss, had agreed that we would produce the *The Course* between us, splitting the cost. But thanks to the "external pressures", he then pulled out.

'And as a result I had to remortgage my house to cover the added costs. I had to find this extra IR£35,000 on my own.' But that wasn't the end of the would-be producer's problems.

The experienced director who Brendan had on board to direct his play pulled out, telling him that *The Course* simply wouldn't work. This was like a red rag to a bull to Brendan, who instead decided to direct the play himself, and had to convince the cast that it would still work.

He had never directed before but that wouldn't stop him.

The PMA that was central to the plot of the play was the very thing that inspired him to make it happen.

Yet right up to opening night, it looked as though he was staring defeat in the face. The box office was deathly quiet. The production hadn't even sold enough tickets to fill the front row of the 600-seat theatre. Anyone else would have pulled the plug there and then. But then they didn't have that unshakeable O'Carroll confidence.

'I thought we were knackered,' says Brendan. 'I thought it was all over. But we had to go on.'

And then a miracle happened – on opening night in October 1995, the people of Dublin flooded in to see his play. The fans of his outrageous stand-up shows wanted to see what the fuss was all about, while others turned up to help him stick two fingers up to the theatre establishment who had shunned him.

'I had misread my audience,' says Brendan. 'They're not people to buy tickets way in advance. They go along on the night.' And so Brendan and his cast walked on stage to a full theatre. 'I made my acting, writing and directing debut all in that night,' he recalls, still proud as punch about the defining moment in his stage career.

And did Dublin like *The Course*? Well of course! They loved every moment, and in particular the irreverent and coarse humour. And they went home and told all their friends and family about this wonderful new play.

It went on to run (after a switch to an even larger theatre) for 18 straight weeks, beating all records for a performance in the city. It outsold all the Festival plays put together.

'At the end of the day, the play ran while the Theatre Festival ran,' he told the *Newcastle Evening Chronicle*. 'It was the only theatre in Dublin that wasn't part of the Festival at that time. Nice to say, we turned over more money than the entire Festival. And, I swear, by sheer coincidence we made in profit exactly the same amount the Festival lost. Instead of running for eight weeks it ran for 18 then moved to another theatre. It went on to become the biggest-selling comedy in Ireland.'

In fact, the 'biggest selling' record would only be broken some years later by his first *Mrs Brown's Boys* play. 'PMA had worked for me,' says Brendan. 'It gave me the confidence to believe I could make it as an entertainer.'

And there was an added bonus. Brendan had written one of the key parts with his sister, Eilish – later to star in *Mrs Brown's Boys* as Winnie McGoogan – in mind. But Eilish wasn't available and the part went to a young Dublin actress, Jennifer Gibney.

Ten years later, Brendan and Jenny would end up married, but we'll come to that later.

'It all worked out the way it was supposed to,' says Brendan, grinning. 'All you have to have is a little positive mental attitude.'

Like with so much of his work, his mother Maureen was watching over him as he came up with the idea of his first play. He jokes that Mum used to call him Heinz 57 because he had so many jobs. One that caught his eye was a newspaper advert which offered 'IR£1,000 a week without working'. It turned out to be selling accident insurance and the company had a PMA course to boost motivation.

The principle behind PMA struck a nerve with Brendan's own natural inclination to turn every 'neggie' into a 'possie'. He mastered the technique so completely that he soon broke the company's record for daily policy sales and when he came to write a play he decided to write one about the course. As well as breaking Irish box office records, *The Course* went on to have a successful tour of Britain before heading to Canada.

Though better known for his potty mouth than his pep talk, PMA would later prove to be another money-maker for Brendan – with a lucrative sideline as a highly paid professional motivator. He became a contracted mentor to big-shot businessmen from Ireland and the United States. As unlikely as it may seem, he was making a fortune by being on call whenever these tycoons needed a source of inspiration to drive their companies forward .

John Douglas, his original PMA instructor, was among his closest friends and they worked together presenting intensive courses for management executives.

For Brendan, PMA is a way of life. 'It's not a psychic thing,' he says. 'It gives you belief in yourself, your kids, the future. It makes you believe that a lot of the shit that's going down can change.'

Brendan is, first and foremost, a businessman. For him, comedy isn't so much a calling as a calling card. He puts the business into show business and Agnes Brown in particular has been built as a brand.

His growing commercial empire would at various times comprise the likes of an advertising agency, a film company, a television production house and an American-based publishing firm specialising in gift books for hotels and airlines.

These days, *Mrs Brown's Boys* is a massive growing brand with all sorts of merchandise and spin-offs being conjured up all the time. He would also boast a property portfolio later as his career really took off.

But for Brendan, there was an element to his work aside from wanting it to be successful, making money and furthering his career. With his working class roots, he hoped his work would open up the theatre to people who had never dreamt of setting foot in one before.

Yes his work was rough and ready, it was snubbed by the Dublin Theatre Festival and some critics. But the public loved it. This would be a common theme throughout his career. And it left the snobbier end of the theatre world choking on their canapés when the 'great unwashed' arrived in their droves to lap up Brendan's bawdy work.

'My introduction to theatre was through pantomime, and I remember one year going to five pantomimes – I was around 11 or 12,' he told *The Irish Times*. 'Theatre has become so serious that unless it's Hedda Gabler or Keely & Du, it doesn't seem to merit entry into the theatre. And I'm not saying that I was determined to change that. I wasn't. But I just went; if I build this, they will come.

'The theatre-going audience of Dublin is a minority but the pubs are being jammed for Sil Fox and Brendan Grace and for small two-piece bands. Now, the theatre people say that the audience is not out there – the audience is out there but you can't introduce a child to reading by giving him *War and Peace*. You've got to give him *Peter Pan* and *Ladybird*.

'Now, I'm not suggesting that that's what I'm doing. What I'm saying is I'm conscious of the fact that the audience I want are out there, and I want to get them into the theatre.

'Most of them are in a theatre for the first time in their lives. They're sitting in the Tivoli theatre, looking around, thinking, this is the London Palladium. The spongy seats and the stage right there happening in front of you! This is the business!

'In a lot of cases, this wasn't their night out that week, this was their night out that month. They got a babysitter, they got a taxi, she got her hair done, he got his suit cleaned and pressed for that night out.

'I'm conscious of the fact that they're out there and they want some entertainment. But there is some theatre that is aimed at highbrow, and highbrow is sometimes too high for me. Willie Russell twigged it, Alan Parker twigged it: If we're going to entertain the audience, we've got to get the audience in the door!'

Brendan insists he wasn't trying to embarrass the Irish theatre by staging *The Course* – quite the opposite. He'd like nothing better than to be acknowledged and welcomed by the very people who tried to halt his stage career before it got going in earnest.

'*The Course* is art whether they like it or not,' he told the *Irish Times*. 'It's art because a mass of people have come, sat down, laughed, thought about this, felt good and went home. It had an effect on them.

'Now, I didn't set out to be an artist, I set out to write something that would entertain people and make them feel good. The Theatre Festival rejected my work but they didn't just reject my work; the fact is they get a lot of work submitted and they have to reject some of it.

'However, I was a good bet: two bestselling novels, popular in his own right, he can pull an audience. But, what would he do to the credibility of the theatre? If we allow this guy who never went to drama school, never went to writing school, didn't go beyond primary school, and we acknowledge him as being a playwright, then all that we stand for, that we support, that we grant aid, becomes redundant.'

Brendan would make many more forays into the United Kingdom with *The Course* and this time victory was his. Audiences loved it, catching on quickly to the unique Dublin humour, while most critics were savvy enough to focus on the play's sheer entertainment value, or at least respect how much the audiences were lapping it up.

In a brilliant piece of back-handed praise, Charles Spencer wrote in the *Daily Telegraph*: 'Examined rationally, this is a dreadful play, shoddily designed, lazily characterised and intellectually dishonest. There is only one problem: it works.'

The Course notched up plenty of possies in London, Manchester and Glasgow and also got a standing ovation in Liverpool.

'I had no intention of going on the stage, ever,' he told *The Scotsman* in 2000. 'I had no thought that I would write. When I found myself out of work, I answered the ads in the paper like everyone else and ended up selling cheap accident insurance policies door-to-door.

'You have to learn a script and deliver it word for word, even the joke at the end. We'll pay you if your leg is broken, we'll even pay you if your heart is broken, no, but seriously...

'The play still works. It hasn't dated. People are still looking for confidence boosters in their life, for encouragement, for endorsement.

'I attended one of these courses once. And I was so amazed by the results and the people I met, that I had to turn the experience into a play.'

Learning to have a Positive Mental Attitude certainly worked for Brendan. It gave him the confidence to go on stage. To write his first book. To write his first play. 'The promise of IR£1,000 a week was my lure, initially,' says Brendan. 'But the fantastic thing about PMA was it gave me the confidence to realise I could do anything.'

'When the Dublin Theatre Festival rejected *The Course*, my confidence was totally shattered,' he told the *Irish Sunday Mirror*. 'I felt very low. But I went to see Steve Collins fight Chris Eubank and watched him as he made his way into the ring. Everyone thought he was going to get battered and I could see him muttering to himself: "I'm still the champ, I'm still the champ."

'He ended up destroying Eubank and I thought, "Fuck it, I'll do the same." And I did.'

CHAPTER 12

MAGGIE THATCHER AND THE TV SHOW

It was a mark of how far this working class boy from a rough Dublin northside patch had come when in January 1996, Brendan was invited to join Nobel Laureate Seamus Heaney at University College Dublin, where the students held an Arts Day to raise funds in aid of the Simon Community, the homeless charity.

From abseiling down buildings to appearing with his old friend Gay Byrne at RTE's *People In Need Telethon* that year, Brendan would always, always make time for charity throughout his career. Things were picking up still on the work front and Brendan bagged his first movie role in *The Van*, based on the book from the Roddy Doyle *Barrytown Trilogy* and a follow-up to the massive success *The Commitments*.

Unlike *The Commitments* though, *The Van* wasn't

critically acclaimed. Yet in what was an early sign of what was to come – Brendan was *The Irish Times* review in May was headlined 'Lack Of Spark From The Van' but noted that 'a fine supporting cast' included Brendan with 'a spot on performance as a wily fixer'.

The Irish premiere at Dublin's Savoy cinema – complete with Bimbo's clapped out red and white chip van outside – would come that November. Leading star Colm Meaney was in the States filming *Star Trek* and missed it but Brendan would be there with future *Harry Potter* actor Brendan Gleeson.

But the biggest names there – though no one knew it back then – were a certain girl band by the name of The Spice Girls. Victoria Beckham and co didn't hang around for the after-party, maybe because it was so informal – there wasn't a black tie in sight – and the supper was, appropriately enough, fish and chips and burgers in Reynards nightclub, where Brendan partied into the wee hours with the likes of Arthur Mathews, writer of *Father Ted*.

He was mixing in the world of showbiz more and more as his career continued to grow, networking and making contacts along the way.

The rise of Brendan on the stand-up circuit in Ireland was well-established by this stage, so to as an author and a playwright, and now his first regular TV break came in 1996 when he landed a role presenting a weekly comedy quiz show on RTE called *Hot Milk and Pepper*. But where did the show's bizarre title come from?

In 1997 Brendan admitted to *Hot Press* magazine that his unlikely inspiration was the late British Prime Minister, Margaret Thatcher.

In his days working as a waiter, during the first EC summit in Dublin in 1984, he was locked in Dublin Castle for four days and four nights and allowed only one phone call home. His job? Margaret Thatcher's personal waiter. Brendan was requested to serve her the unusual drink concoction of hot milk and pepper. He later learnt that it was a cure for constipation.

'I looked after Mrs Thatcher's every need for four days and nights,' he boasted to *Hot Press*.

'I brought Mrs Thatcher hot milk and pepper, would you believe? And she was in her dressing gown at the time. It was 4am and she was still at work, papers all over the place.

'I'd been introduced to her for the first time in Aras An Uachtarain [The Irish Presidential home] when she arrived: "This is Brendan, he will be looking after you during your stay." "Oh," she said, "so wonderful to meet you. Do you have a wife and family, Brendan?" I told her I was married to Doreen and had two kids then, Daniel and Fiona.

"Oh, that's lovely," she said. "We won t keep you too long away from those." She wanted an Irish whiskey. I got her a Gold Label and she put a drop of water in it.

'She always called me Brendan, always very polite, never snappy. On the last day, four days after the introduction, when I brought her out a cup of coffee and Geoffrey Howe a gin and tonic, she said, "Well, Brendan, you can go home to Doreen, Fiona and Daniel now." The woman was a fucking pro.'

During the same period that he was hired as a waiter by the Department of Foreign Affairs he served many other world leaders. 'Robert Mugabe was something scary,' he says. 'He walked in surrounded by his ministers and cohorts, and you never saw a group of people who looked more like a gang of thugs in your life.'

Brendan told the *Evening Herald* paper in April 2013, after Baroness Thatcher's death, how he gave Maggie her first taste of Irish whiskey. 'The first thing Mrs Thatcher said to me when she got out of the helicopter was that she wanted an Irish whiskey. She said it was her first time in Ireland and she had always wanted to try an Irish whiskey.'

Brendan told the paper he had already made his mind up about the British leader before he met her: 'I didn't like her. Being from a strong trade union family, a Labour family, I wasn't predisposed to like her, but at the same time, I was very professional in my gig and tried to look after her the best I could.

'I can remember being woken up one night by Mrs Thatcher's M15 security team, who told me that the prime minister wanted hot milk and pepper in her apartment. I brought it down to her, and years later when RTE offered me a quiz show and asked what I should call it, I said *Hot Milk And Pepper* after Mrs T.'

Brendan would cram shooting the 28 half-hour shows – six months' worth of episodes – between appearing in Dublin's Gaiety Theatre in *The Course*. After years struggling for recognition, he was now going to be a regular fixture on the TV screens in homes across Ireland.

'It's a fabulous feeling to be 40, and at long last I have finally figured out what's important to me,' he would say.

Brendan's potential as a future TV star was spotted then by *Hot Milk and Pepper* producer Gerald Heffernan of Frontier Films.

'He's an absolute joy to work with,' said Gerald. 'Down

to earth, fiercely intelligent and a natural born comedian. He's a new TV star in the making.'

Word of his hilarious warm-up routines would spread around RTE's Montrose complex, with staff dropping in to catch him in action during their breaks.

The show featured two teams of four competing each week, answering a series of related questions. 'All of human life passes through here,' said Brendan. 'Firemen, singers, pilots. Today we have four models against four Clare hurlers. Later on we'll have four jockeys up against four disc jockeys. It's hilarious.' The show was co-hosted by Brendan's long-time stage partner Gerry Browne, who tried to keep things on an even keel and contain the madness.

Around the same time that his new TV show was announced in July 1996 it was revealed Hollywood had plans for a big screen adaptation of *The Mammy*, with shooting scheduled for the next year and he was offered a year-long run for *The Course* in London's West End at the Shaftesbury Theatre.

'They want to open in October after we came back from a month in Canada,' said Gerry Browne at the time. 'But myself and Brendan may have to step out of it because we have commitments to filming *The Mammy*.'

It also meant the pair would drop plans for *The Course* to open in New York in October, but Brendan wasn't disappointed: 'Boy, am I glad. I see off-Broadway shows are selling an average of 170 tickets a week. That means 20 punters a show. It'd be easier to give them all their money back and tell them each a joke.'

There was an early indication that Brendan was comedy's 'Mr Marmite' – you either love him or you hate him – for despite rip-roaring success in the UK and Ireland, *The Course* bombed in Canada, where it received scathing reviews by critics who couldn't get to grips with the Dublin humour and bad language.

Kate Taylor from *The Globe and Mail* gave it one-star review and said rather than a comedy it was 'a mystery – a mystery why this puffed-up skit that seems to think it's a play enjoyed enthusiastic reviews and full houses in Dublin, where it played a whole five months at the Tivoli Theatre before touring Ireland and England.

'Maybe the Irish are starved for laughs. Maybe there's something funny in Dublin's drinking water. Maybe there's a great pub right next door to the Tivoli. Or maybe the key to the mystery has something to do with O'Carroll's popularity as a comic on television, video and radio as well as the author of two novels.

'Perhaps the Irish love him so much, they would buy tickets to hear him read the Dublin phone book.'

Because *The Course* had played to packed houses in Ireland and Britain, Brendan was advised to move his show to a bigger venue in Toronto because it was being staged at the same time as the local film festival was screening *The Van*.

'*The Van* was pulled from the film festival and we were left high and dry,' he explained.

The Canada reviews hit ticket sales very hard and Brendan admitted to the *Irish Daily Mirror* in October that it had flopped in Canada: the production lost $50,000 during its four-week run in Toronto.

'Nobody knew who I was and we didn't sell enough seats, it was as simple as that,' said Brendan. 'We had terrible trouble with local unions who wouldn't allow our crew to move as much as a light bulb. In the end I decided on damage limitation. Now I just want to put the experience behind me.'

It was the one blip in an otherwise good year for Brendan. One of his fiercest critics to his stand-up, stage and TV work throughout his career would be *The Irish Times*. Yet one indisputable fact the paper could not challenge, was Brendan's success as an author on and 19 October, they reported on the success of the third book in his trilogy, under the headline 'What Big Talents You Have!'

'You can be as snooty and as culturally superior as you like but there's no doubting that Brendan O'Carroll playwright, author and stand up comedian, is a phenomenal success,' the paper conceded.

'On Wednesday night he launched his new novel, *The Granny*, in Reynards. *The Granny*'s initial print run is a staggering 65,000, for a lot of Irish books 10,000 would be considered a wildly optimistic run.'

By December 1996, after such a successful and busy year, Brendan was being dubbed 'the comic who can't sit still' in the Irish press, with a TV show, comedy gigs, charity work, stage plays and his work on a new movie based on his hit book *The Mammy*, with Angelica Huston, in the pipeline.

But, despite the large number of 'possies' in Brendan's life at that moment, there were still a few 'neggies' lurking in the wings. He was enjoying success on a string of fronts and working his socks off, as he had been the past three years, and it was putting an inevitable strain on his marriage. The first signs that there might have been problems at home came on 29 August 1996 when he was guest-editing the *Irish Daily Mirror*'s showbiz column.

Brendan saw similarities in what he was experiencing at home with the TV host Eamonn Holmes, whose marriage to his first wife Gabrielle Holmes would end in divorce. 'I really feel for Eamonn and Gabrielle Holmes,' he wrote. 'I know little about their marriage, apart from what I've read. But I do know how difficult it is to keep two lives on an even keel.

'Like Gabrielle and Eamonn, Doreen and I met when we were youngsters. In 1977 Doreen married a waiter. And for the next 15 years I *was* that waiter. It's very difficult for her to adjust to what is happening in our lives.

'I love my work with a passion and, although I'm happy to say it provides an income for my family, essentially I do it for my own gratification. Doreen balances that with constant reminders of life in the real world, like turfing me out of bed at half past eight of a Wednesday morning to put out the dustbins (I don't think the bin-man is even up at that time).'

But just as things were going so well, another personal blow would hit the O'Carrolls. As *The Course* prepared for the second leg of its Irish tour, Doreen was back in hospital with a new health scare, a setback in her battle against the breast cancer which had been casting a shadow over their lives for the past few years.

As the opening night in Mullingar approached, Doreen developed an infection after having breast reconstruction. The show must go own has always been Brendan's adage, and so it did, but every day he would drive to the hospital to check that his wife was coping with her recovery.

Like Agnes Brown herself, Doreen lived for her home and family and, according to Brendan, the meteoric rise of his career never once seemed to impress her: 'Doreen is completely underwhelmed by what's going on in our lives,' he told the *Irish Times* in 1996. 'I remember the opening night of my one-man show at the Olympia in Dublin – Doreen couldn't make it because she was taking her mother to the bingo.

'I come in, having sold out the Lyric Theatre in London's West End, and I get "oh, that's nice". Fiona comes in with a B in Maths and it's celebration time.'

Brendan secretly hoped that it was Doreen's quiet belief in him that meant she didn't need to be there to share in his triumphs. 'That's really it,' agrees Brendan. 'Doreen's attitude always was that Brendan will think of something.'

He recalls the times when they were penniless and the dole money would run out. "She'd say, "ahh, you'll think of something" and the thing is, I did!"

But these were the early signs that their marriage might not last, as Brendan's new life in showbiz was not something that Doreen could get to grips with. Brendan said at the time that it felt like he was standing on the edge of the Grand Canyon – but there was no one there beside him to share the exquisite view.

CHAPTER 13

LILY THE PINK

Buoyed by the runaway success of *The Course* and with the TV quiz show increasing his profile even more, Brendan began 1997 full of ideas and full of beans.

His first one-man show, called *The Story So Far*, had a week-long run at Dublin's Olympia theatre in January. Even *The Irish Times* – who have never been flag-wavers for Brendan throughout his career – were unusually generous in their review.

'Pitched somewhere between "outrageous and nostalgia laden", Brendan O'Carroll's first one-man show is as much as you would expect from the performer – ribald tales shot through with scatological reference, and with the odd glance back at Dublin in the "rare oul' times".

'O'Carroll's near to phenomenal popularity is based

around knowing his audience as well as he knows his material. But he's obviously a very accomplished performer who knows a thing or three about working a stage.

'Based on his veering between the expected and perhaps not so expected in this show, it will be interesting to see where he will take his material from here. What the public expects and what Brendan O'Carroll desires may not be one and the same thing.'

What they couldn't have known then though was that Brendan was honing his skills all the time, gaining experience in what would work and what wouldn't. He was making it his business to discover what his audiences loved so that he could give it to them in spades.

There was no stopping his rise in popularity and in February he appeared at an Amnesty International Benefit concert at the Gaiety, billed as the 'largest ever collection of Irish comedy talent'.

Brendan shared the stage and more than held his own with the likes of Dylan Moran, Jason Byrne, and *Father Ted*'s Dermot Morgan and Pauline McLynn. But not everyone appreciated Brendan's sharp tongue though, and his quick mouth got him into trouble when he found himself on the wrong side of the law in April 1997.

A civil case was settled out of court at Waterford Circuit Court after Brendan had a run-in with a traffic cop. The policeman claimed that Brendan had abused him outside Dungarvan District Court when he was prosecuting him for breaking the speed limit. He had taken exception to remarks as the comedian left the building.

A statement was read in court to Judge Sean O'Leary saying that the parties had accepted there was a misunderstanding which had now been resolved to everybody's satisfaction. To be fair, it was out of character for Brendan, who has throughout his career worked tirelessly for charity and never forgotten his roots.

With a background growing up in working class areas of Dublin and a mother who was a politician who fought to help the disadvantaged, perhaps it was inevitable that Brendan would consistently give something back despite the trappings of fame.

In 1997 he made time in his busy diary to speak at inner-city meetings of anti-drugs activists and visit schools round the country deterring youngsters from taking the likes of ecstasy, cocaine and heroin. They included Finglas, where Brendan and Gerry both grew up and where they were patrons of the local Drugs and Aids Forum.

At the same time, Brendan, then 41, was raising money for the famous Coolmine Therapeutic Community in Dublin – a treatment centre for helping people overcome addiction – and said he saw there the lives blighted by drugs.

'They are caught in a trap. Often they want just a friendly word or a joke and then the words of hope which mean they won't give up the fight.'

He also met the other victims – the addicts' relatives. Brendan said: 'When you have an addict in a family, the entire family is affected by it. It is hard to find words to describe how their world falls apart. As a comedian, I have never admitted this before, but when I have met some of them I have cried and cried and cried.'

Brendan started by talking to teenagers at schools while touring with *The Course*. He said: 'I start off with a few jokes to get through to them. Then I tell them those involved in drugs are total idiots. It gets rid of any suggestion of glamour or excitement about drugs, because teenagers don't want to be thought of as stupid. I explain the exuberance of being young and alive is the greatest drug you can have.'

Brendan told the *Irish Sun* of the secret heartache behind his campaign – more than 100 people he knew had died from drug abuse. He said: 'They were all friends and acquaintances. Some were childhood mates – I know so many that have died. They came from decent hard-working families. It's heartbreaking to think of all the tragedy and misery.

'It's one of the main reasons I got involved. Families are being torn apart and communities devastated. Look at all the lives that are being destroyed. The message has to go out that drugs kill – it's as simple as that.'

In December that year Brendan told the *Irish People* that he and Gerry were organising a massive anti-drugs campaign at Dublin's Point arena the following March, featuring pop stars Boyzone along with players from the Irish football squad.

The celebrities would invite 7,000 children aged 11 and 12 to pledge to stay off drugs in a show called *High on Life*. Brendan, who would host the Point show, said: 'We are trying to make it something the children will never forget. Any kid sitting in his kitchen can tell his mammy he will not touch drugs. But groups of kids making the pledge together may have a more lasting effect.

'Recent statistics show 90 per cent of kids who take drugs for the first time are with friends. Peer pressure is the biggest factor in drug-taking. We want the kids to talk to their heroes and realise that drugs aren't cool.'

Brendan gave a certificate to every youngster making the pledge at the show.

'You have to give something back to the community otherwise what you get in life is of no value,' he said.

Mrs Browne by this stage had been a success on radio and in novels, but she had yet to be developed in the flesh for stage or TV, but Brendan's voracious appetite to create new works would not relent; ideas were flowing all the time, and it did not take him long to finish his second comedy play, *Grandad's Sure That Lily's Still Alive*, about six rebellious pensioners in an OAP home, which made its debut in Dublin at the end of June, 1997.

'Everybody thinks that there is no such thing as sex after you're 60,' said Brendan. 'But that is a load of old rubbish. I want to show that there is sex not only after 60 but after 70 too.'

He may well have been gleaning tips when he joined Paul O'Grady, famous for his alter-ego Lily Savage, at a party in Dublin that June, but Brendan showed his first signs of performing in drag by starring in *Grandad's Sure That Lily's Still Alive* as randy pensioner Maisie. The plot revolved around a resident called Grandad who sets out to track down the Lily of the title – a lady of the night he encountered decades ago.

But once again Brendan had to take a risk financially, and needed business partner Gerry to do the same. He directed and starred in the play while Gerry produced it, but the pair were stumped when they needed to raise production costs of IR£115,000. Finally they remortgaged their houses to finance the production, putting up both their homes as collateral.

But the comics' shocked wives didn't see the joke when they failed to tell them first about the financial arrangements, despite being taken out for a slap-up Chinese meal to soften the blow. 'The women kept asking "Why have you brought us out for no reason?"' said Gerry. 'They were horrified when we told them.' Brendan revealed how Doreen had cried for an hour afterwards: 'She rushed off to light a few candles in church.'

'My wife has got used to the idea now of remortgaging our home,' said Brendan at the time. 'But I have had non-stop sleepless nights ever since. I know exactly how I will feel if there is a standing ovation on the first night – "Thank God, my house is safe".'

The play would kick off on a 10-week run in the Gaiety on 30 June and thankfully for Brendan, Gerry and their families, the gamble just about paid off. It wasn't as big a hit as *The Course* but it wiped its face financially, even though it got mixed reviews from the critics.

The Irish Times said: 'Brendan O'Carroll's second play is sure to annoy the snobs, but it's also guaranteed to entertain the crowd almost as much as its wildly successful predecessor, *The Course*. Once again, O'Carroll goes for the cheap laugh, peppering his script with flatulent lavatory humour and throwing in plenty of f-words to pump up the dialogue; and, once again, the narrative drive is sacrificed to the name of a good gag.

'There's nothing like a good "shite" joke to get things off to a flying start, and before we even know the character we're already laughing like Father Jack in the ladies' loo. Who cares if Lily's still alive – we just want to know when the next double entendre is coming.

The Times said: 'At its base, the play is an Irish re-working of *One Flew Over the Cuckoo's Nest*, with the action transferred to an old people's home. The setting is a clever stroke, allowing O'Carroll to buffer the shock value of his smut by having it voiced by pensioners.

'Letting loose salvo after salvo of crude humour against the backdrop of the grim netherworld of a retirement home offers an appealingly complex texture to what is, at a very obvious level, a scatological workout, in which characters debate such questions as the difference between sounds made at orgasm and those made on the lavatory.'

Even in the face of his own financial worries, Brendan never got greedy. Bearing in mind he had to remortgage his house to get the production off the ground, he still made sure to hand over the profits of one of his performances to charity.

It's something he would do time and again in his career and on 14 August 1997 he gave all the proceeds from one show to the HIV/AIDS unit in St James Hospital. 'A lot of people seem to think HIV and AIDS are other people's problems,' he said. 'It's been forgotten about to a large extent, so we're more than happy to help out.'

Brendan explained the background to his gesture to the *Irish Sun* was in fact that a friend's AIDS death spurred him on to raise money for medical research. Scots-born mime artist Thom McGinty, 42 – also known as The Diceman – had died in Dublin two years previously.

'Thom was one of the first people I met when I started trying to get into showbiz,' said Brendan. 'He was such a great bloke and he was really generous with his time. Like a lot of people, I was absolutely devastated by his death... In some ways, AIDS is becoming the forgotten illness. But it is still devastating lives and families here in Ireland. It's vital that there is enough money to try to help patients and find new forms of treatment.'

The play went down well with the punters in Ireland and Brendan told Gerry and the rest of the cast it was time to take it to the UK.

It was a tried and tested strategy that he would adopt all his career: create a hit play, pack them out in Ireland, then head for the UK before – if it was a big success – taking it global.

Just as he had with *The Course*, Brendan decided on Liverpool's Neptune Theatre as the perfect place to start. He was popular there, so what could possibly go wrong?

They had barely set foot on English soil at Liverpool's Speke airport when all hell broke loose with screaming and shouting and a scrap at the police checkpoint at arrivals. Brendan couldn't believe it when he turned to see his partner Gerry Browne being wrestled to the ground by three cops.

It all kicked off when Gerry took exception to filling in an immigration form because he was Irish. It ended with him being arrested and accused of assaulting a policeman.

'I asked her if Scots also had to fill in the form and she pointed to a Prevention of Terrorism sign on the wall,' says Gerry.

'She asked me if I had a problem with it and I told her I had.'

Gerry alleged the officer demanded the form and put her hand on his shoulder. He says he brushed it off and was promptly arrested by three other police. He claimed he was taken to a holding cell where, he alleged, the cops assaulted him.

THE MAN WHO IS MRS. BROWN

He later received hospital treatment for cuts to his head and ears and bruising to his back. Gerry claimed one of the policemen called him 'fucking Irish scum' and a 'Paddy bastard' during the incident, which lasted about 15 minutes.

'It was a nightmare. I'm a big guy from Finglas, 6ft-1in and 14 stone but I've never been so scared in my life.'

He was taken from Speke Airport to Belle Vale police station in Liverpool where he was interviewed, fingerprinted and photographed.

'I wanted to get out so I pleaded guilty to get away in time to do the show. My mortgage is riding on it. I was allowed to leave with a caution.'

Brendan, meanwhile, was allowed through the checkpoint after completing the immigration form and rushed to contact the Irish Consul and a solicitor.

'There is no way we are going to let them get away with this,' said Brendan. 'What they did was an utter disgrace. You should see the state he's in. I can hardly believe it.'

Brendan insisted it was ridiculous for anyone to suggest his pal was capable of violence. 'He is the nicest bloke you could meet – a big old sugar plum,' he said. 'It's been a terrible ordeal for everyone. Gerry's wife was distraught when she heard what had happened.'

The show would go on for Brendan and Gerry despite their ordeal but after opening night they were threatening to pull their hit show out of Liverpool.

Brendan told the *Irish Daily Mirror*: 'Gerry is in a lot of pain with his neck. He's finding it terribly difficult to continue with the show. He's in agony on stage and can barely move with the pain. It's killing us all to see him in such agony.

'We've decided that if he doesn't improve by Friday we're going to pull the play and take everybody home to Dublin. That will mean 21 people out of work because of this terrible incident.'

The Police Complaints Commission investigated the incident after Gerry made a formal complaint but it moved on to become a diplomatic issue.

Gerry and Brendan intended to challenge the legality of travellers being forced to fill in immigration forms when journeying between Ireland and Britain and TD Proinsias de Rossa, leader of the Democratic Left, raised the question in the Dail.

Brendan had close links there, through his mum's political past and he himself having fronted an election broadcast video for the Democratic Left at the end of May 1997.

The Irish Times reported that Mr De Rossa said: 'It is quite unacceptable that what originated as no more than a minor disagreement should have been escalated by the police into what amounted to a serious assault on an Irish citizen. As far as I know, the Irish alone of European nationalities are asked to complete the cards, and they are certainly contrary to the EU principle of freedom of movement.'

The Minister of State for Foreign Affairs, Liz O'Donnell, said the Government was 'particularly concerned at suggestions of anti-Irish prejudice and behaviour' and that the Home Office was aware of the seriousness with which the Minister, Mr Burke, viewed the matter.

Gerry was so upset by the sorry episode that he vowed to sue over it and claimed Brendan was ready to as well for financial losses. The Liverpool run of *Grandad's Sure Lily's*

Still Alive had to be cut short, and plans to take the production to Mayo and Tipperary were scrapped.

Gerry explained: 'This has cost us a fortune. I just haven't been up to appearing. I am still receiving treatment for the injury to my neck and my hearing has also been affected.'

Gerry estimated he and Brendan lost at least IR£25,000 and as much as IR£50,000 as a result. But he added, 'This court action is not so much about money. The people who did what they did to me should not be allowed to get away with it. This sort of thing seems to happen to a lot of Irish people and I have absolutely no intention of letting this matter rest until I get justice.'

Gerry Browne said later he regretted he didn't in fact pursue the case further, but he simply couldn't afford to: 'I just ran out of money on it. At that stage things were very bad so I couldn't pursue it – I should've and I've been sorry I didn't – but I couldn't afford to.'

There was to be a Hollywood movie made of his book *The Mammy*, but in true fashion Brendan didn't want to stop there.

He announced in October 1997 ambitious plans to make three more movies in just two years, adaptations of his plays – *The Course* and *Grandad's Sure Lily's Still Alive* – as well as one based on his new novel *Sparrow's Trap*.

All three would be made by Brendan's own company Little Mo Productions, he said. Brendan revealed, 'It's going to be some two years for us. Angelica Huston is definitely directing and starring in *The Mammy*. She's going to give me a small part in it and Gerry Browne is producing it. But apart from that, it's her baby.'

And while he was treading the boards by night in Liverpool's Neptune Theatre with *Grandad's Sure Lily's Still Alive* before it was cut short, by day Brendan was feverishly finishing off his fourth book *Sparrow's Trap*, the story of a boxer who has one last shot at the big time, which would hit the shelves in time for Christmas.

He said he was putting stand-up comedy on the back burner until at least 1999. 'I'll come back and fill the Point Theatre then. I feel I have to move on from all that, but I'll definitely go back to stand-up someday because I love it and it's how I got my break in show business.'

Former Olympic runner Eamon Coughlan turned up to launch *Sparrow's Trap* (later to be renamed *The Scrapper*) in Drumm's Emporium that October. The ink was barely dry on the book as Brendan steamrolled ahead with the movie, revealing more plans at the launch: 'I'm hoping to get Stephen Rea to play the lead role and I'll probably have a small part in it myself.' The movie would be produced by Brendan's stage and TV partner Gerry, who would play a character called Froggy.

With Brendan being a relentless creative force, his mind would always be overflowing with new ideas. Some would get produced and with the ones that did, almost always they would prove to be a huge success, be it novels, plays or whatever.

Some wouldn't get off the ground – like a radio comedy series *Northside Blues*, a movie called the *Bingo Hall Gang* and many others. He has even spoken of plans of publishing a book on his mother's diaries.

One project that went close to production was a chat show. In January 1998 RTE liked the thought of giving the livewire comic the chance to front a talk show to fill the three-month void during the summer when the *Late Late Show* is off-air. The irony would not be lost that just five years after appearing on the *Late Late* and making a name for himself, here he was with the chance to stand in for it.

Brendan filmed the pilot for the proposed new show and he chose motormouth broadcaster Eamon Dunphy and boxer Steve Collins as his guests for the pilot show, filmed in Dublin's Tivoli Theatre. Gerry said: 'It was real hairy, with close-to-the-bone interviews. Brendan had Dunphy talking about his divorce and other personal matters.'

He described the format as being close to that of legendary US chat show host Jay Leno. Like Leno, it used a live studio band which Gerry would front if they got the green light from RTE. But the pilot wasn't liked by the men at the top, leaving Brendan and Gerry disappointed at coming so close.

Another source of frustration would be a sitcom set in a bar called Foley's (the same name as the pub in the *Agnes Browne* trilogy and *Mrs Brown's Boys*). The BBC were reportedly interested – so much so that Candida Julian-Jones, producer of *Birds of a Feather* and *Red Dwarf*, flew to Dublin for talks with Brendan and Gerry over it.

Gerry said at the time: 'She has told us she wants enough material to fill an eight-part series to start off with. If it goes ahead – as we expect it to – we will start work immediately. This is a great break for myself and Brendan.'

But it too would be another near miss as a deal would not be struck. He would have to put his dreams of having a UK television show to one side – for now.

CHAPTER 14

AGNES BROWNE THE MOVIE

In New York on 20 May 1998, the official announcement was made that October Films had acquired worldwide rights to Brendan's book *The Mammy*. Brendan could scarcely believe this was happening.

Anjelica Huston, who won an Oscar for *Prizzi's Honor*, was to direct and star with Jim Sheridan, who had won fame for *My Left Foot* and who had brought the book to Anjelica's attention, named co-producer.

'Jim Sheridan told me about it,' said Anjelica. 'The script is tremendously engaging. It has great curves. Brendan does this rare thing of combining street comedy with very poignant stuff, the rollercoaster between comedy and tragedy happens a lot and it's really intriguing to play.'

Set in Dublin in 1967, *The Mammy* was billed as 'a warm

111

and funny story of a feisty young widow, Agnes Browne, who, with her seven children, gamely faces life's adversities following the death of her husband'.

'This material is perfect for the very talented Anjelica Huston to direct and act in,' said October Films in a statement. 'Anjelica and Jim each have a wonderful sense of Irish culture. We are thrilled to be working with them both and look forward to a fantastic film.'

Jim Sheridan said it had a 'wonderful script' while Anjelica Huston announced, 'I am interested only in directing projects to which I have a very strong connection, this script touched me in a very powerful way. I am very excited about this project.'

Three days later Huston and Sheridan took to a platform in the grounds of Planet Hollywood in Cannes during the Cannes Festival to announce in person their plans for *The Mammy*, which would be scripted by Brendan.

'As far as I know, this will be the first time a woman has ever directed herself in a feature film,' observed Jim Sheridan. Shooting was scheduled to begin shooting in Dublin that summer. But it would end up beset with problems before, during and after production.

The lead role of Agnes Browne was originally supposed to be played by Rosie O'Donnell, but she had to pull out as she was busy after adopting a baby, forcing Anjelica to take it on herself. 'I only stepped in as actress at the last moment because Rosie O'Donnell dropped out,' she said. 'I was disappointed but rather than lose the film – because we didn't have the time to recast – I stepped in. I wouldn't have done that had I not been compelled to.'

Anjelica hoped for better luck with the male lead in the

movie, with Frenchman Gerard Depardieu lined up. 'He's got a very tight schedule, but he would love to do it,' she said. 'The role is a French baker who's opening a shop in the markets in Dublin.' But Depardieu had a motorcycle accident, ruling him out and a relatively unknown actor took the role instead.

Then there were furious rows between Jim Sheridan and Brendan, with Anjelica caught in the middle, about how the movie plot should develop. Brendan was writing the screenplay and Gerry was co-producing. Both were to star in it as well, but Gerry lost his part after breaking his leg and Brendan almost forgot about himself.

'I was very pleased with the script, then I read it again and thought, "Fuck, there's no fucking part in it for me", so I wrote myself in.'

Brendan would play 'Seamus the drunk' in the film and would have few lines but it would be another indication of his talent as a character actor – Anjelica liked Seamus's part so much she expanded it.

'Anywhere we have a street scene she has him in there,' said Brendan. 'He's walking or stumbling around. He's a comical character and it's now a fairly decent role, which is great for me.'

He also arranged that Dublin actress Jennifer Gibney, now his second wife, would have a small role in the film as well.

There was also a problem with the title. To an American audience, *The Mammy* sounded like a Deep South plantation story, so it had to be changed. Brendan and Anjelica first decided to call it *The Irish Mammy* before it was ultimately called *Agnes Browne*.

113

'When our assistant brought the film in at the JFK Airport, he got some bad looks when they saw the title. They didn't like it,' Anjelica said. '*The Mammy* translates into mother; Irish children have called their mothers mammy, but the connotations in America are different. The consensus was it was about Aunt Jemima and that was a danger and a pitfall I didn't want to fall into.'

And when it came out, while the movie had garnered fans it was largely pilloried by reviewers for being cheesy, clichéd and over-sentimental. 'Oirish stew' was what one newspaper called it.

In the book Agnes dreams of meeting Cliff Richard, but for the film Tom Jones was drafted in to appeal to the US audience. But as the movie was set in 1967, this drew more ire from critics when the singer appeared as his modern-day self.

And on top of it all, the movie was sold to another company before its release. 'It was kind of lost in the shuffle of a company,' Anjelica told the *Sunday Times*. 'I made it for October Films, which sold to USA Films before the film was released. And when that happens, often it's better for the studio that inherits the film, profit-wise, to write it off.

'And so I would say the release was really not a good one. We opened a few days before the Academy awards in an envelope [small] theatre where they didn't even put the title up outside. So my disappointment was immense in terms of how that film was ultimately treated.' According to USA Films, the budget for *Agnes Browne* was 'under $20million'.

It wasn't all bad, however. When the movie, which also starred Ray Winstone, was screened the following year at Cannes it drew a standing ovation.

'The thing about Angelica Huston is that from the very first time she read the book she got it, she got the essence of it,' says Brendan who was full of praise for Anjelica overall, but there were plenty of disagreements in the making of the movie.

'The film I wrote is not the film that's going to come out,' Brendan said at one stage, upset at how Huston's romanticised and sentimental adaptation for Hollywood was distorting his book and screenplay. She had lived in Ireland during the 1960s but the Ireland she remembered was rural Galway, not the rough and tumble of inner city Dublin.

'But Huston's involvement had helped secure financial investment from America for the movie, so perhaps inevitably that meant it would be made primarily for an American audience.

'I wrote the book and screenplay from a position of first-hand knowledge,' Brendan told the *Sunday Times*. 'But Anjelica saw it in American movie terms. Then, you have an English art department, an English director of photography, an American editor and so on. Somewhere in there the pieces that made the book work have got lost.

'One look at the set and I could see the film was no longer about Moore Street. Anjelica had created a completely new market, a compromise between a west of Ireland horse fair and Petticoat Lane in London.

'In one scene she has a ceilidh band playing outside a pub in Moore Street. If we'd seen a ceilidh band on Moore Street in 1967, we'd have set them on fire for the craic, just to see how quick they could play.

'The Chieftains are doing the score but 1967 Dublin was more rock 'n' roll. It was more a part of Britain than

Ireland. It was Tom Jones, Herman's Hermits, miniskirts. It wasn't the Chieftains. But that's not the way the director saw it.'

Yet Brendan's most hard-fought struggles on *The Mammy* were not with Americans but with fellow Dubliner Jim Sheridan, whose production company made the film and who co-wrote several of what became 15 screenplay drafts.

'Jim and I did not become friends,' says Brendan. 'I haven't seen or heard from him since the last day of the shoot. We're very different people with different views of life. He slammed down the script once at a meeting and said: "This positive attitude of yours makes me sick." I tend to look on the bright side. Jim's much darker.

'He didn't really like my screenplay. He's very much into subtext and there wasn't enough subtext for him. There certainly wasn't enough confrontation in it. Jim wanted the mother and the eldest son to be fighting all the time. But that's not what happens with mothers and eldest sons. Mothers and eldest daughters, sure. At the script meetings, we were only short of throwing chairs at each other.'

The fractious relationship between Brendan and Sheridan reached breaking point in Los Angeles as they argued over the final drafts. 'By the middle of the week, my head was numb,' says Brendan. 'Jim is a very, very dominant man. I spent so much time with my back to the wall, fighting with him to retain parts of the script, that I became exhausted. I decided to just become his typist, to type whatever he wanted.

'A couple of days later, I e-mailed it to Anjelica. She was livid. She rang me and I'll never forget her words. She said:

"You little bastard. I send you over there with *It's A Wonderful Life* and you send me back *Some Mother's Left Foot*. Where is my movie?" I laughed and gave her Jim's mobile number.'

In order to duplicate the film's 1960s-era Market Street setting (which stood in for the real Moore Street Market), Huston and her crew used a street in the city's less-developed Ringsend area. Anjelica told the *Los Angeles Times* that the locals were less than impressed by the arrival in their midst of a Hollywood movie star.

'Not one bit,' Huston recalled with a rueful laugh. 'We were allowed to use this one street, as long as the merchants there were able to keep working. And when we were still working on Friday nights, they didn't like it one bit, because we were stopping them from having a good time at the end of the week. We'd be trying to shoot, and the singing would start to get very, very loud in the pubs.

'I was stuck in the booth in the ladies room and scared to come out, because there were two women there just slagging myself and Brendan O'Carroll off to such a degree, I was ashamed to show my face.'

'They were a bit scalded that they couldn't play their bingo,' recollects Marion O'Dwyer, who played Agnes' best friend Marion Monks in the film.

Anjelica was also given a fright when she went undercover on Moore Street with Marion to research their roles. The market traders 'called the cops on us for working without a licence', said Anjelica, who saw the funny side afterwards.

Boyzone star Stephen Gately, who would tragically die in 2009 aged just 33, was offered a role in the film.

Brendan's spokesman Rory Cowan said in February 1998, 'Everybody thinks Steve is ideal for the part.'

Gately's manager, pop impresario Louis Walsh, added, 'Steve's delighted to be offered the part and we're now trying to work things out so it can fit into his Boyzone schedule. But it's a fantastic opportunity for him.'

He didn't star in the end but legendary Welsh crooner Tom Jones, these days a judge on hit TV reality show *The Voice UK*, got Brendan all emotional during filming – he broke down in tears when Tom spoke the lines he had written to Hollywood superstar Anjelica.

'I cried,' says Brendan. 'I just cried. I was sitting in the front row of the Gaiety Theatre and I think a lot of the people there cried as well, because the way he said it was just so moving.'

In the scene, Tom looks up from the stage to Anjelica, playing Agnes Browne, and says, 'You know, I believe that sometimes this turbulent and tragic world turns on its head and comes to a sudden stop, just to accommodate somebody's dream. This song is for a dreamer. Dream on Agnes Browne, for all our sakes, dream on.'

'I remembered typing those words at four o'clock in the morning in my house,' says Brendan. 'And here was Tom Jones saying them to Anjelica Huston. I couldn't believe it was happening there in front of me. It was all too much for me and the tears just came.'

Despite their differences, Brendan developed a good bond with Anjelica during filming and in July threw a rooftop party for her at his penthouse pad in Temple Bar – the heart of Dublin's social life, packed with bars and restaurants – and perhaps another sign that things were not well at home.

He hired a karaoke machine to make sure the night went with a swing and they drank and sang until 5am. And in spite of how sentimental the film would be, and how demanding Anjelica could be on set, Brendan was still full of admiration for her.

'I love Anjelica to bits,' he told the *Irish Mirror* in 1999, adding that she was 'very hurt' by claims that he felt she had ruined the movie she starred in and directed.

'Myself and Anjelica are great friends. In a newspaper interview I had only pointed out that the movie would not be the same as the book – but it shouldn't be.

'She said to me, "Brendan, you're breaking my heart", but it's all sorted out now. She knows I am delighted with the movie. Anjelica Huston is a director with grit. Anjelica is a perfectionist – if that is what it takes to make a masterpiece of my book, then so be it.'

Anjelica also dismissed reports that she, Brendan and producer Jim Sheridan had fallen out during shooting. She said: 'Brendan actually kept everybody's spirits up, he was on the set even when he wasn't needed for filming. He is electric in terms of his energy. But it was very difficult for me jumping in and out of scenes. When I came on set every morning the actors were all sitting there waiting for direction from me.'

But Anjelica was proud of the end product, as she told the *Boston Herald*: 'It has in it the essence of a fairytale. And there's an optimism to this story, it's about a survivor and a courageous woman. But it harkens back to a more innocent time and certainly in terms of the way I was feeling about Ireland when I made the film, a bittersweet nostalgia.'

In 1999 the film would be chosen to close the prestigious Cannes Film Festival for its world premiere, which a 'thrilled' Brendan hailed as 'a great honour'. He would miss it though, as he was in the States, as well as missing the Irish premiere at the Galway Film Festival because he was on stage in Glasgow. But he cleared his diary for the opening night in Dublin.

In general the movie opened to mixed reviews in the States and the UK in March 2000. While it won praise in some quarters, the overriding opinion that it was cheesy, clichéd and sentimental.

The Los Angeles Times called it 'high corn', adding, 'Huston is a sucker for sentiment, and Agnes Browne is a sap's holiday'. *Irish Times* critic Michael Dwyer said: 'Anjelica Huston's simplistic and sentimental film' offered "a thick slice of screen Oirishness".

'This trite movie is suffused with an enforced jollity and a Rare Ould Times phoniness that's exemplified by Paddy Moloney's so wistful score and the shots of little girls doing their jigs and reels in the street to the accompaniment of whiskery musicians.

'Much more grating, however, is O'Carroll's characteristically crude humour, which is jarring in the context. Those attempts at comedy derive from mispronouncing "ejaculate" as "evacuate" and "orgasm" as "organism".'

The Times said Anjelica had ended 'up with Guinness all over her face' and added, 'it's a vanity box. Having spent a large chunk of her youth in Ireland, Huston is no stranger to the comic tics of Dublin life, so frankly she should be lynched for directing a theme park ride as appalling as this.'

The Independent said, 'Agnes Browne is a pretty indigestible slice of Oirish Twaddle... I'm only surprised the film-makers didn't think of sending on a bunch of leprechauns as a support act.'

But while it was savaged by the broadsheets, the tabloids seemed to love it – a general theme that would be present throughout Brendan's career. In his *Daily Mirror* column, the film critic and TV host Jonathan Ross called it a 'sensitive and often very funny drama'. He added, 'The costumes and production are faultless and this film is bursting with rich humour, only occasionally venturing into corny territory.'

And under the headline 'Golden Browne', Mariella Frostrup wrote in the *News of the World*: 'A stunning performance from Anjelica Huston and a surprise appearance from hip-swivelling singing legend Tom Jones are the highlights of *Agnes Browne*. As well as being a bit of a tear-jerker, this film is entertaining and funny, with a great cast, including the ever-impressive Ray Winstone. This is a film for everyone, with one ultimate message – love is all you need.'

CHAPTER 15

CAUGHT IN A SPARROW'S TRAP

Enthusiasm, as the no-hopers on *The Course* were told, is one of the three ingredients in PMA. And Brendan O'Carroll's enthusiasm has never been in doubt throughout his career. But in 1998, as he spun the plates of his busy career, he became over-ambitious and stretched himself too far – sending things crashing to the floor.

What with best-selling novels, packed out plays and stand-up gigs, a top TV show and a movie adaptation of *The Mammy*, Brendan seemed like he could do no wrong. He was the man with the Midas touch and would later admit he had become arrogant. He thought he was bullet proof.

And when he took on the enormous challenge of making his own movie, *Sparrow's Trap*, based on his novel of the same name, there were disastrous consequences.

Sparrow's Trap tells the story of Dublin featherweight Sparrow McCabe, played in the film by Brendan, who floors the challenger for the world title. But he walks away before delivering the final punch that would make him a champion and drifts into the underworld, becoming a fugitive after witnessing a killing.

Gerry Browne was to play his pal Froggy, the only man Sparrow can trust, alongside RTE regular Simon Young and model Vivienne Connolly, who had both been given their acting debuts in Brendan's play *The Course* two years earlier.

There was a role too for *Brookside* baddie Bryan Murray, who would play a policeman, and Brendan had hoped – through his boxing pal Steve Collins – to get Prince Naseem Hamed to film a key scene, but the idea fell through.

The plan was to release the following autumn after being premiered at the Toronto Film Festival in September that year. It would never happen. The troubles on *Sparrow* were strictly financial. That February, Brendan and Gerry had gone for broke when they splashed out IR£2.2million on the biggest gamble of their lives.

But it was a gamble that left Brendan on the brink of another financial disaster. The movie backers pulled out at the last minute, leaving the pair with a debt of half a million pounds.

'Once that happened we had to pay for everything ourselves and myself and Gerry remortgaged our houses in order to get the cash,' says Brendan. But because of Brendan's enthusiasm, or perhaps bloody-mindedness, they pushed on with filming.

Brendan's daughter Fiona, then just 17 years old, had a part in the film and he later told the *Irish Mirror* that he was in tears during filming of her scenes which involved two thugs breaking into her house, shooting her husband and beating her up while her baby is crying in an upstairs bedroom.

He said: 'My eyes filled up with tears when I realised it was my own daughter they were slapping around the place while she cried out for help. There wasn't a dry eye on the set. It was harrowing to hear her crying out.'

Fiona had pestered her dad into giving her the part in the movie, having read the screenplay when he left it lying around the house. She had no screen or stage experience apart from studying drama at school for a year. She said: 'I was very nervous at first but dad was very supportive.' Keeping it a family affair, Brendan's son Danny, then 14, also had a walk-on part in the movie.

Then three weeks before the end of principal photography, Brendan and Gerry ran out of money after a complicated dispute with an Irish production company, also involving *The Mammy*, which ended up before the courts.

'If I have to get down on my hands and knees for the next two years, everybody will be paid,' said Brendan at the time to the *Sunday Times*. 'The two currencies upon which the movie business trades are fear and greed. I'm not afraid of them and I was never greedy. Litigation holds everything up, but it doesn't scare me. Every penny me and Gerry have was put into that movie so we will finish it. And *Sparrow's Trap* will be a better movie than *The Mammy*.'

A desperate Brendan told the *Irish Sunday Mirror* at the time that he hoped to rescue a deal with a new distributor:

'Now we are working on a deal with the distributors Buena Vista. We were let down at the last minute and part of it was due to our naiveté. We thought we had a deal which was cut and dried but it fell through. I'll make damn sure in the future that everything is set in stone before I invest that much money in a deal. I'm learning hard lessons about the movie world – but I'm learning fast.

'Both me and Gerry remortgaged our houses to raise the money for this deal. I wasn't too bad, but Gerry had already remortgaged his home to build a new house so he's living like the television character Petrocelli in a place with one door and two windows!

'Buena Vista has offered us a deal and RTE has made a generous offer for the television rights. But we are in a Catch 22 situation because the Buena Vista deal depends on us having the finances and we still need to find another IR£250,000 from somewhere.

'So at the moment Gerry is trying to get that by visiting as many friendly bank managers as possible. But I'm confident that it will come through. I've know Gerry since we were lads. I have never found another person who has so much confidence in me. If I said to Gerry that I wanted to paint the Moon green, he'd say: "Right, I'll go out and price the paint." That's the kind of support I get from him. He's an incredible friend.'

The failure of the film was a hard lesson for Brendan. As his mum could have told him, pride goes before a fall.

'Thanks to the film I spent three years in court,' he told the *Northern Echo.* 'Not fighting anything, but just so that people could consolidate their debt. I would just go in and say "yes, that's right" and then I'd make an arrangement to pay it off this way or that way.

'But, do you know, it's funny because it was a great catalyst for me as well. Sometimes you need a good kick in the backside and what happened to me was I had this fantastic appearance on *The Late Late Show* .

'The day after that, everyone in Ireland knew my name. All of a sudden, you start to believe that you are the person on the bloody poster.

'That's what happened to me. Six or seven months later I started to believe that if I wrote out my shopping list and I put it on the stage it would be a hit. So I really felt invincible. It was a hard, expensive lesson for me.

'When I started to make *Sparrow's Trap*, I had a fantastic distributor and two days before we started shooting I lost him, which means I lost my funding.

'Instead of turning up on the set and saying "bad news guys, the movie is off", my pride and stupidity made me feel I couldn't let everyone down and I'd promised everyone seven weeks work. I just started making the movie without any money. We'd shoot from 7am to 7pm and then I'd go out every night to try and raise the money and then I'd go back to shooting.'

At one stage the 112 crew on the movie had to go without some of their wages.

'Every time the phone went it was almost always to do with money – bills, bills and more bills,' Brendan told the *Irish Mirror*. 'I had hocked everything I ever owned. My partner, Gerry Browne, did the same. We were known as The Borrowers but this was no children's story – this was very real and very frightening. I should have stopped right then and there, but I didn't. The ego was so big I thought someone would pick it up.'

A defiant and ever-positive Brendan told people at the time that he was confident he'd fix things: 'I'm not that worried. I'll always be able to put food on the table and educate my kids.'

Brendan claimed that RTE were buying the TV rights to the movie for IR£100,000 and that as he finished editing the film he would sell the rights in up to 20 other countries to cover the debts.

'I believe this film is good enough to pay its way. I held a sneak preview of it in a Dublin pub last week and the crowd loved it.'

Brendan's infectious enthusiasm allied with how much people loved him and believed in him meant that friends were only too happy to lend him money to help out.

Even the security company working on the film stopped sending in invoices when they heard of the financial problems he was facing. And Brendan was stunned when they then offered to invest IR£25,000 in the movie. But making the movie was ultimately a harrowing experience for Brendan, who was forced to come up with IR£70,000 a week to pay the bills during the six-week shoot on location in Dublin.

Point Theatre owner Harry Crosbie also bailed him out by going guarantor on his overdraft. And in the end Brendan brought *Sparrow's Trap* in IR£300,000 under budget. 'We also finished three days ahead of schedule and I managed to return 40 rolls of film to our suppliers,' he said afterwards. 'I think this movie will open a lot of people's eyes and show them what can be done for IR£2.2million.'

Brendan and Gerry didn't draw a wage for months, instead living off their savings, which eventually ran out. Brendan said, 'Gerry and I have put every penny we have – and even a few we don't have – into it. Everything is at risk, including our homes.'

A schedule of payments was then set up to help them pay off some of their debts with suppliers, crew and others involved in the movie. They owed a fortune to friends and creditors and faced ruin if the movie flopped.

Brendan admitted to the *Irish Sun*: 'We have debts that we can't cover unless we sell the movie at the right price. I've heard rumours that I am bankrupt – actually at the moment they're very close.'

Sparrow's Trap sadly proved an intolerable strain on his partnership with Gerry Browne, the boyhood friend who encouraged and bankrolled Brendan's initial foray into show business.

'We had different ideas on what we wanted Brendan O'Carroll, the product, to do,' he says. 'I wanted to develop things – plays, films, businesses – that would make money when I wasn't working. He wanted to stick with the stand-up, which was making a lot of money but was too gruelling for me. We agreed to differ. Things petered out more than busted up.'

They finally went their separate ways in 2000, but it was the spectre of *Sparrow's Trap* that prompted it.

'Trying to make a movie cost me IR£2.2m and I had IR£30,000 in the bank at the time, so I had to borrow all around me,' said Brendan in 2011. 'Would you believe me if I told you I only paid off the last of the money last March?'

He told Australian TV Channel Seven's current affairs programme *Sunday Night*: 'It was terrifying. Two days in a row I sat in the apartment I was living in, didn't turn on the lights, all the curtains pulled, and sat in the dark. For two days. Didn't eat, didn't drink, just sat in the dark for two days.'

Brendan had lost all his self-confidence – and sank into a depression. Even those with a belief in PMA and a normally unshakeable self-belief can have their down moments. He was so low that he was feeling that he could no longer be funny.

He told the *Irish Sun*: 'I was in the depths of despair for a while. To be honest, I didn't even feel like being funny. My confidence took a huge knock. I only acted in the film *The Mammy* for the cash, and after that I had no work at all lined up. It was a bad time for me.

'But somewhere down the line I realised that I could still be funny. So I pulled myself out of it and got back to work. Now I'm working and being funny again, and I've never been happier in my life. Maybe you need a big knock to realise that it is a wonderful world.

'Life is not about falling down, it's about getting back up on your feet.'

Brendan is honest to a fault – and he gave another typically candid interview to Radio Ulster's Stephen Nolan in 2011 when he spoke at length about the *Sparrow's Trap* calamity on *The Nolan Show*:

'It actually was never a flop,' he said, 'because it was never released. Albeit expensive, it was a great, great lesson for me, because this is the second time round, kind of, for me... The time comes for you, no matter what age you're at, where you get that first flush of success in your life, when you start to believe that you really are the person on the poster, when you start to believe you really are what people are writing about you.

'You completely lose the run of yourself. And you get to the stage where you think, you know I actually don't need a bridge across the Liffey, I could walk on that water. And that's basically what happened to me. I was naive.'

Nolan asked Brendan if he had become arrogant at this time. 'Oh God yes,' admitted Brendan. 'Never nasty, thank God, but you don't realise it at the time. I believed that whatever I did would work. That there was absolutely no possibility that it would fail. I don't think that's necessarily a bad thing, I think you should be going into any project you're going into with that attitude.

'So instead of just going in with a positive attitude and "this is going to work", which is not a bad thing, you also throw caution to the wind. I borrowed and I scraped while I was making the movie and over the following 12 weeks made the best movie I could make, and it's actually a cracking little movie.

'Nobody's ever seen it, it's here on my shelf edited, finished and it's never been broadcast, and the reason for that is that it's taken all those years to pay off the debt.

'I spent IR£2.2million on it but not only that, IR£1.5million of which I didn't have, that didn't belong to me, so I ... spent the next six, seven years paying back the debts of that. I wouldn't release that movie because it wasn't my movie, until the debts were paid it didn't feel like my movie, and I only finished paying it off quite recently in the last 18 months.

'You have to remember at the time Stephen, I always believed, and I still believe, that I'm a good guy, I'm a good hearted person, I look in the mirror and I see a good guy. I contribute wherever I can; I try to make people's lives better around me, so essentially you know you're a good guy. So you don't think that anything like that can happen to you.

'It's only in retrospect that you look back and go, "My God, that was so stupid of me. Why did I think that that would happen? Why did I think that that would work? Oh God, you idiot."

To this day, *Sparrow's Trap* is gathering dust in Brendan's home, unseen by the public at large. Although you wouldn't put it past Brendan to either get it released eventually, or plan a new blockbuster remake.

But as Brendan admits now, that calamity and its IR£2.2million debt was the best thing that ever happened to him. In despair as to how he would pay it off, he locked himself alone in a hotel room. For two days he just sat there. On the third night, he knelt down beside the bed and prayed for help, not to God, but to his mother.

'I had a dream, vivid as could be,' he told the *Toronto Star*. 'I had an office and a secretary and she said "Your mother's on the line."

'I picked up the phone and Mum said, "I got your message, son. If it's worth getting down on your knees to pray, then it's worth getting up off your ass and doing something about it, son."

He did. His solution was to turn Mrs Brown into a popular stage character in a series of astonishingly

131

successful plays which would lead to a TV series and now plans for a movie.

'You see what I mean?' he says, 'I owe everything, and I mean everything, to my mother.'

With his positive outlook in life Brendan can look back now and see the benefits of near financial ruin – even though it would take him more than a decade to clear his debts, it prompted the creation of *Mrs Brown's Boys* the play to save the day.

CHAPTER 16

'MY MARRIAGE IS OVER'

Roars of laughter erupted from a corner of the bar in
Oscar Madison's pub in Kinsale where Brendan
O'Carroll was holding court. Not for the first time he was
the centre of attention, but this time he was celebrating his
43rd birthday in the company of Dublin actress Jennifer
Gibney, and was in flying form.

The drinks were flowing and, panatela cigar in hand,
Brendan was having the time of his life.

But he was blissfully unaware that lurking in another
corner of the bar was a reporter and photographer from the
Irish News of the World watching his every move.

They had been snooping on the pair for days and were
following their every move, tracking them all the way from
Dublin to the picturesque County Cork seaside village.

They were watching the day before as Brendan played golf at the scenic Old Kinsale Head club. They reported how he had flown from Dublin to Cork and that Gibney had 'followed by train to spend the night with him'.

The newspapermen were sitting over a pint as they saw Brendan, carrying his golf clubs, with Gerry Browne and other friends arrive at the bar. Satisfied that they had enough on him, they called him up and asked him to comment.

Things were about to come crashing around Brendan's ears as the lid on his private life was blown wide open and the break-up of his marriage revealed. To make matters worse, the newspaper alleged that he had been having an affair, with Jenny cast as 'the other woman'.

On 20 September 1998, the *Irish News of the World's* front page splash screamed 'Brendan O'Carroll in secret 2-year affair' with the heart-crushing second headline: 'Dates as wife is at Lourdes'.

'Ireland's top comic Brendan O'Carroll has admitted living a double life which he kept secret from his fans,' the story ran. 'He dated blonde Jenny Gibney while his wife Doreen went to Lourdes to thank God for saving her life from cancer.

'Now Brendan, who met Jenny two years ago, has opened his heart to the *News of the World* and admitted his marriage is on the rocks. He said: "We just went in separate directions."'

For their inside spread the tabloid ran the suggestive and salacious headline: 'At midnight in the B&B Jenny gave star a big birthday kiss – comic admits going on trip with blonde.' The story claimed Brendan and Jenny had shared

Brendan O'Carroll brandishes the award for Best Situation Comedy for *Mrs Brown's Boys* at the BAFTA Television Awards 2012.

© *Doug Peters/ EMPICS Entertainment*

Above left: Maureen O'Carroll, Brendan's mother, who was a big influence in th comedian's life. © *Photo courtesy of Independent News & Me*

Above right: Brendan O'Carroll presenting his *Hot Milk and Pepper* TV quiz sho © *Photo courtesy of Independent News & Me*

Below left: Anjelica Huston (left) who played Agnes Browne in the film *Agnes Browne*, with co-star Marion O'Dwyer. © *Photo courtesy of Independent News & Me*

Below right: Brendan O'Carroll holds a copy of his book *The Chisellers*, one of trilogy of Agnes Browne stories. © *Photo courtesy of Independent News & Me*

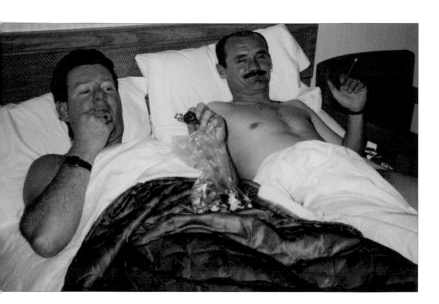

ove: Echoes of Morecambe and Wise: Brendan O'Carroll in bed with his long-
~~e~~ friend and stage partner Gerry Browne (left) in Edinburgh during their 1992
~~K~~ tour.
© *Photo courtesy of Gerry Browne*

ow: Brendan O'Carroll with Gay Byrne and market trader Margaret Gannon
~~D~~ublin's Moore Street Market which strongly influenced the creation of
~~s~~ Brown.
© *Photo courtesy of Independent News & Media*

Above: Brendan O'Carroll takes it easy after collecting the Best Entertainment IFTA for *Mrs Brown's Boys* in 2012.　© *Photo courtesy the Irish Film & Television Academy*

Below: Brendan O'Carroll and the cast of *Good Mourning Mrs Brown* celebrating the news that *Mrs Brown's Boys* had been nominated for a BAFTA

© *Collins Photos, Du...*

endan O'Carroll and his old friend the comedian Peter Kay at the opening
ght of *For the Love of Mrs Brown* at the Olympia in Dublin.

Left: Brendan O'Carroll in character as Mrs Brown in the stage play, *Good Mourning Mrs Brown*.

© *Collins Photos, Dub*

Right: Brendan O'Carroll with TV presenter Gay Byrne (top) and radio presenter Joe Duffy (middle) at the launch of RTE's People in Need Telethon.

© *Photo courtesy of Independent News & Media*

ove: Brendan O'Carroll with his son Danny, who plays Buster Brady in *Mrs Brown's Boys*, at a fund-raising golf match for the Irish charity, Charity 25.

low: Brendan O'Carroll and his wife Jennifer Gibney with the Best Situation Comedy Award for *Mrs Brown's Boys* at the 2013 National Television Awards.

Above: Brendan O'Carroll with his son Eric who played Bono, Mrs Brown's grandson, in Brendan's videos of *Mrs Brown's Boys*.

Below: Brendan O'Carroll and the whole cast of *Mrs Brown's Boys* after winni the BAFTA for Best Situation Comedy in 2012.

a 'loving kiss' before retiring to their IR£40-a-night double room together.

The paper also alleged that Brendan and Jenny had 'been dating while wife Doreen battled against breast cancer' and said she had 'visited Lourdes to thank God for saving her from the disease'.

Brendan was quoted telling the paper: 'I can't say that I wasn't with Jenny in Kinsale because I was. It sounds horrible though, it makes it all sound so sordid which it is not. Jenny Gibney is an assistant director. She has directed my videos, she is a very good person, she's an actress. Of course I see her, but I also see about 20 other women.

'My wife has been to Lourdes, yes. But she is clear of cancer now, thank God. Doreen and I have been separated for two years but we are not separated on a nasty basis.

'We didn't have a fight or a row. It's the pressure of this business. I do not want to make Doreen look a fool, as though she is losing her man to another woman... it is not like that. I still love Doreen and she still loves me. She is the mother of my children and my wife of 22 years.

'When you are an artist – and I am an artist – and you are out and about, your greatest wish is for everybody to know you. That's what you are trying to achieve. But for Doreen that's not what you are trying to achieve when you marry a waiter, and she married a waiter. She feels she is living in a goldfish bowl, the show business didn't gel with her.

'So I bought the apartment I have in Temple Bar two years ago. But it has been great that when Doreen goes away I have been able to stay at her home in Ashbourne and mind the kids. It's also been great that my daughter Fiona could come and stay in the apartment when she is at school.

'Jenny has been a great support to both of us, not just me. All of my friends have been a great support. Doreen doesn't want to say anything. We have been trying to keep it private because we figured it's private business, family business. It is not because of Jenny that we've separated, it's because of the pressures of show business. She would be at home lonely and I would be away lonely. The two of us just went in different directions.'

Brendan revealed the circumstances of first meeting Jenny in an interview with the *Late Late Show's* Ryan Tubridy in 2011, explaining how he had gone to see a play because he was interested in using the director for his own first play. 'I wanted to look at this director's work and Jenny was in the play,' he said. 'I told the director I was coming to see it on the opening night. I was late coming back on a flight from London so I rang ahead to the box office and I said "Look, don't let my tickets go." And they said "No, the director told us to hold this curtain till you get here."

'So I thought "Oh Jesus" and I felt more under pressure. It was supposed to start at eight, so I got to the theatre at 10 past eight, into the box office, "I'm so sorry, I'm really sorry". They gave me the tickets and I went in the corridor and there was a girl standing outside the door, I said "I'm really sorry I'm late" and she said "Just effing sit down."

I said "That's no way for an usherette to talk." Anyway, I got me seat and the lights went down and the usherette walked down and she got on the stage – she was an actress. Now what I didn't know was that it was Jenny. What I didn't know was that nobody told her the curtain was being delayed.

'And she'd to make her entrance from that part of the stage outside; she was out there 20 minutes crapping herself. So I was no help. So anyway, I watched it that night and I thought he probably won't be directing, as we had a different sense of comedy – but I'll have his barman and I'll have his barmaid, and Jenny was the barmaid. So I approached her and Jenny came and joined the show.'

On the whole, 1998 was not a great year for Brendan O'Carroll. It was the year that *Agnes Browne* the movie was filmed, but it received mixed reviews and Brendan himself was disappointed in the final product adapted from his first novel.

Then there was the disastrous decisions made over *Sparrow's Trap*, his own bid to make a movie of another of his books which would leave him in financial ruin and on the brink of bankruptcy and depression.

No, it wasn't his best year in the world of showbiz, and the tabloid exposé on the break-up of his 22-year marriage to childhood sweetheart Doreen just made matters worse.

'Every Saturday night for two years I checked the Sunday papers to make sure there was nothing in them about us,' Brendan commented to the *Sunday Times*. 'I'd ring Doreen and tell her there wasn't. I enjoyed making those Saturday night calls, telling her everything was okay. But I can see it's also better that we don't have to pretend any more.

'The newspaper story hurt Doreen and that's what angered me. It was her dislike of publicity that made us drift apart in the first place. I wanted to take on the world and I became a workaholic. Doreen wanted me to be a normal husband doing husbandy things. I brought chaos into her life.'

They would remain close and Brendan would say in 1999 that he had no intention of ever marrying again. Six years later, of course, his view on that would change.

Forever honest about the ups and downs in his life, Brendan talked frankly about the heartbreak of his marriage break-up in an appearance on *The Late Late Show* shortly after the newspaper revelations.

He said he still regarded his wedding to wife Doreen in July 1977 as the happiest of his life. But the star, who thrived on publicity for years while his wife remained notoriously private, said they just grew apart.

'I was married at 21 and separated by 42 and they were both turning points,' he said. 'Everything runs its course but they were some of the best years of my life. I enjoyed every one of them. But worlds grow apart, people change and people want to go in different directions.'

It says much about the man that despite the lurid headlines splashed across the *Irish News of the World*, that very same day he turned up for a charity event. The Sport Against Racism Ireland (SARI) fundraiser saw a match between two celebrity teams, one headed by Curtis Fleming of Middlesbrough and Ireland, the other by Brendan.

The next day, in an interview with the *Irish Mirror*, he said his wife was his 'best friend' and that they still had a great family life. Brendan insisted that his relationship with actress Jennifer Gibney, as alluded to by the *Irish News of the World*, wasn't the reason for his marriage break-up.

'My marriage didn't split up because of Jennifer. I go out

with Jennifer but I also go out with other women. Myself and Doreen go out with different people and it's perfectly fine. We didn't hurt each other in all of this. We just sat down one day and decided we were going in completely different directions. We kept it to ourselves because we didn't think it was anybody else's business. The kids knew and our family knew and we thought that was enough. Nobody was trying to hide anything but we're quite relieved now that the whole thing is out in the open.'

As with most couples going through a break-up, their thoughts turned to how it would affect their kids. Their youngest child Eric was only six when the story came out and in an interview *Sunday Independent* alongside his dad in 2004, when he was 12, he said that he encouraged his parent to reconcile their marriage.

'All I remember,' said Eric, 'Is we were all out in the car and Dad stopped for the paper and the front said "Brendan and Doreen O'Carroll Split". I told them you have to not stop talking and I tried to get them back together a few times.'

After the split, their other son Danny went to live with Brendan and eventually Eric followed but would later share his time between Doreen and Brendan and have two of everything, lots of friends at both homes and a good relationship with Jenny when she later became his dad's new partner.

'We never separated, not me and him,' says Brendan of Eric, who would later play Bono, Mrs Brown's grandson, in his father's videos.

'I'm very proud of him,' said Brendan in the *Sunday Independent* interview. 'And I'd be lost without him. He started off 2lbs 5oz and I can't believe what he's become.

He started off a little bag of sugar and turned out a big bag of ah...'

Laughing so he nearly fell over, the paper reported, Eric finished off the word for his father – the bad word, of course. Like father, like son, in so many ways.

But splitting up was good for the family, Brendan would argue, although he later admitted to his old friend Gay Byrne, on his TV show *The Meaning of Life*, that he did in fact feel guilty over the break-up of his marriage.

'Oh God yeah, you do,' confessed Brendan. 'First of all the manner in which we broke up. I would rather it had happened earlier. That I had been more honest. I was also very arrogant. I thought, "well I can't leave because she'll just fall apart", which was terribly selfish and arrogant of me, she's far from fell apart, she's extremely happy and living with a lovely guy.

'But I could've done it earlier, so I'm sorry I delayed that, I'm sorry I held her life up. And as well as that, I just wish it hadn't happened for the kids. That doesn't mean I was going to not make it happen, I just wish it didn't happen.

'Jenny was in my life at that stage, and certainly there was a perception that I was leaving Doreen for Jenny, which couldn't have been more wrong. I was leaving because I just needed to try and find some kind of happiness and some kind of peace.

'The fact that I did fall in love with Jenny was amazing. And here we are now, what, 15 years later and I'm remarried and absolutely head over heels. I tell you something, God sent her to me. Someone looked down on me and said, "that little... needs a minder". And he sent her to me. I'm blessed.'

CHAPTER 17

MRS BROWN'S BOYS TO THE RESCUE

The secret of Brendan's marriage collapse was out in the open, but if anything that was more of a relief. He no longer had to live a lie in public.

Agnes Browne the movie wasn't the worst thing that could have happened either. It wasn't a blockbuster hit or much loved by critics but it wasn't a complete disaster and it did his reputation and profile no harm. His books were still doing well, that remained constant, as did his stage work and in particular *The Course*.

He said, 'I had reached a stage in 1998 where everything I touched succeeded – if I was to write a shopping list, I would be convinced it would be a bestseller.' The collapse of his movie project *Sparrow's Trap* brought him back to earth with an almighty thud, but Brendan would never take that ultimate, drastic measure to file for bankruptcy. He would see that as taking the easy way out and it would hurt his pride too much. Besides, he was a fighter, he believed in PMA and he wanted to bounce back.

'I spent a couple of days getting depressed and feeling sorry for myself and then Dennis Desmond of MCD contacted me and arranged a business meeting with one of his associates. They asked me to scribble a play for Dublin's Gaiety Theatre in four weeks time.' Brendan told them he couldn't put it on as it would cost IR£38,000 and he was penniless.

But they offered to lend him the money and all he had to do was come up with a winning play in four weeks. And it was then that he hit on the idea of turning the Mrs Browne radio character into a play. He couldn't believe why he hadn't thought of it earlier, but thanks to Agnes he would catapult back rather than merely bounce.

Agnes would be the person to ride to the rescue and save the day for Brendan, but in the process she would shed the final 'e' in her surname as if to mark a new chapter in her creator's life. And so 'Mrs Brown', the entertainment phenomenon we know today, was born.

The writing came fast and furious and he could, of course, also draw from material that worked in the radio series seven years previously. Writing comes easy to him, he says, often dreaming entire scenes of plays in bed, which makes it so much quicker to scribble them down in his waking hours.

He says he wrote *Mrs Brown's Boys – The Last Wedding* in a morning. He was at his typewriter by 5am and concluded the last of 120 pages before noon. 'Mind you,' he says, 'I had been thinking about the play for six days and I dreamt a few completed scenes, which helped speed it up.'

Assembling the cast was next and he turned to tried and trusted friends such as Simon Young, Gerry and Jenny for the first production. And when the time came to take Mrs Brown from being a radio play to the stage there was only one choice to play the starring role – Brendan himself.

'It was a big leap,' he admitted to the *Newcastle Journal*. I knew I could get away with the voice, but I thought it might ruin it if people saw it was me. I decided to give it a go and got the make-up guy to make me look like Mrs Brown, but I didn't want any mirrors while he was working. I just wanted to see it when it was finished, and when I did I thought I was looking at my mother.

'It took a bit of getting used to, but the audiences seemed to love it and I've been playing her ever since.'

Brendan gave credit to the make-up artist responsible for the face of Mrs Brown in an interview with Mark Lawson on BBC Radio 4. 'It's a peculiar thing,' he said, 'she was such as success on radio and when it came to put a face to Mrs Brown I was very nervous, because it's like reading a book. I have an idea when I'm reading a book... I have a picture of that character in my head.

'And when you see the movie and it's not that character, it's disappointing. So I got a great young make-up artist, he was just finishing college, Tom McAnerney. He knew the radio series and I said, "Tom I want you to make me up what you think Mrs Brown looks like. Don't give me a mirror until it's finished."

'And then when I turn and look in the mirror, if I don't see Mrs Brown I'm not doing this. I turned and looked in the mirror and I saw Mrs Brown. I didn't see my sisters, I didn't see my mam, I saw Mrs Brown and he got it spot on. I gave her the bad hip, that dragging hip, and I got that from an auntie of mine, but Tom gave me the face and the mole.

'The only rule I do have is that she doesn't leave the studio. You won't be seeing Mrs Brown turning on the Christmas lights on Oxford Street or you won't see Mrs Brown opening a store. She doesn't leave the studio and I think that's the best thing for her. But when we're doing the show, listen it's only an act.'

Apart from the voice and her appearance, the key to the character was her walk. With that perfected, he finally walked towards a full-length mirror in full make-up and costume and realised he was looking at his fictional creation, Mrs Brown, made flesh.

The play centred on Brendan as Mrs Brown preparing for the wedding of her young son Trevor (Michael Anthony Byrne) to Maria (Sheila Carthy), daughter of posh Mrs Nicholson (Claire Mullan). Meanwhile her eldest son Mark (Ciaran McMahon) has just been thrown out by his wife Betty (Eveanna O'Meara).

Mark's younger brother Dermot (Simon Young) is a robber, and the remaining brother Rory (Derrick Reddin) is attracted to his friend Dino (Gerry Browne), but is afraid to tell the mammy his 'secret'; sister Cathy (Jennifer Gibney) meanwhile lays claim to being a psychologist.

'I was the first Dublin writer to premiere a Dublin play in the capital in 85 years,' he says with justifiable pride. 'It was a hit at the Gaiety then toured the country.' But Brendan needed to discover if his foul mouthed matriarch would travel. Could she attract an audience outside of Dublin?

On opening night in Cork in January 1999, in costume as Agnes, he addressed the rest of the cast. 'It's now in the lap of the gods and the audience,' he told them.

'Everything was riding on that show and we killed them,' said Brendan later. The stage legend of Mrs Brown had truly been born.

Yet in an surprise gesture – considering his ongoing financial problems – kind-hearted Brendan and his partner Gerry Browne pledged to donate all the profits from the 'world premiere' to the Chernobyl Children's Project charity.

Just two weeks after opening, it was already being talked about as heading for a West End Run.

English 'scouts' went to Cork to see the show and reportedly said it was one of the funniest plays they had ever seen. 'They are all biting: The Lyric, The Shaftesbury and Chichester theatres all want to talk to us,' Gerry told the cast. 'This is the big break we've always wanted. I believe it can be a West End smash.'

But Brendan admitted he was nervous about Hollywood star Anjelica Huston seeing him play Mrs Brown so soon after her playing the same role in her Hollywood movie. 'I'm sure she's not too happy about me playing the same part before her film comes out,' he said.

Not everyone loved it, of course. David Nowlan of *The Irish Times* gave a savage review of the Gaiety Theatre performance, but he did concede that the audience loved it and it would likely play to packed houses:

Brendan O'Carroll's latest oeuvre is gross, crass, coarse and without a trace of wit. Yet it won laugh upon laugh from its large and enthusiastic audience with every four-letter word, every 'funny' walk, every toilet reference and every mention of knickers. The roaring, shouting and sustained applause at the end came as no surprise: a great many people had had a rattling good night out.

Despite inept direction by the author, and an almost total failure to maintain any narrative drive, the show romped home on waves of squeals and laughs to a rapturous reception. It seems set to pack out its five-week run.

While *Mrs Brown's Boys* was lifting Brendan back on his feet, he was, as always, fighting his financial problems on various fronts.

His books were selling well and he was lined up for a promotional tour in the States, the plays were packing out theatres and Brendan would also land a movie role, playing the part of an undertaker in Alan Parker's movie adaptation of *Angela's Ashes*, the Pulitzer-Prize winning book by Frank McCourt.

It presented another opportunity for him so he immediately said yes, but he hadn't prepared himself for the emotional strain it was going to have on him, bringing back memories of the death of his own son in 1989.

Brendan admitted to the *Scottish Sun* that he had actually cried along with actor Robert Carlyle when they filmed the scenes 'burying children in their little white coffins'. 'Normally in a movie, the poignant moments can be quite hard to do,' he said, 'but it came like second nature to me because there was no way I could stop thinking about my poor wee Brendan.'

Brendan also landed a cameo role as Rissolli in 1999 in the Brendan Gleeson movie *Sweety Barrett*.

In April that year, Brendan made the amazing claim to the *Irish Daily Mirror* that he had 'healing hands'. The paper reported how Brendan was convinced this remarkable gift helped his wife overcome breast cancer in 1992 and, four years later, helped his friend and press agent Rory Cowan beat a life-threatening brain tumour.

'They both had to have radical surgery,' Brendan said. 'But no one could say if they would ever be cured. When Doreen discovered she had breast cancer I thought we'd never make it through but I'd heard about positive energy helping healing. We were terrified but we did our best to remain positive. We were determined she wouldn't give in.

'I had been told by spiritualist Joyce Rawlings that I had a great aura and gave off healing vibes. I had always been told my hands were very warm and dry and she explained that the heat was energy which I could use to help people heal themselves.

'So when Doreen got sick I knew I had to give it a go. After the operation to remove the tumour I placed my hands on her chest and started praying like mad. We were worried the cancer would return but we pushed those fears to the back of our minds and I carried on putting my hands on her. After loads of tests Doreen got the final all-clear and I knew we had worked a miracle.'

He said that he wasn't claiming that he had ever cured anyone – rather, he gave them confidence to cure themselves. Here was his unshakeable belief in PMA coming to the fore again.

He explained: 'If you hurt yourself or have a headache, the most natural thing to do is put your hands where it hurts. We can all do it. What I do is really use it and channel the energy by concentrating and visualising.'

When his friend Rory Cowan was told he had a brain tumour, Brendan encouraged him to face it with a positive mental attitude, and, he told the *Irish Mirror*, 'I knew in my heart he was going to be OK and I kept telling him that. It was difficult for him because he was the one it was happening to. But I think the positive mental attitude I used with him helped.'

Brendan added: 'I put my hands on his head and prayed. I said the Our Father over and over. I prayed that any pain Rory had would be transferred to me so I could help him and share it. The pain thing didn't work so the poor fella had to suffer agonies by himself, but he says the heat from my hands had a magical effect on him. He felt he was healing a little bit more every time.' After tests and an operation the tumour turned out to be benign. Rory recovered and went back to work on the day he left hospital.

'I didn't cure Rory,' Brendan told the paper. 'The doctors didn't cure him. He cured himself. The doctors helped him by removing the tumour and I helped him by sending him positive healing.

'It's all about having a positive attitude. If you think things are going to go wrong they invariably will, but if you think they're going to go right and you work hard to make that happen then it will. But you have to believe.'

Brendan believes that anyone has it in them to be an actor, and he gave his daughter Fiona her first introduction to

Mrs Brown's Boys in April 1999 for one night only at the Gaiety, stepping in for Sheila Carthy who couldn't make the performance that night. When Fiona was older she would end up making the role her own in the plays and hit TV series.

Brendan was thrilled at the early prospect of acting onstage alongside his only daughter. 'I'll see her in a wedding dress for the first time. That's scary! It's funny, I get to be the father of the bride and her mother-in-law in one go.'

As the Cork and Dublin runs would show, success for the play in Ireland would be a given across the country, and Brendan's rambling routines about everyday family life and childhood would go on to strike a nerve with audiences all over the world.

But he would prove especially popular early on in working class cities Glasgow and Liverpool, both with big Irish communities as well, where *Mrs Brown's Boys* quickly became a massive hit with phenomenal sales. But success didn't come easily.

Initially, no impresarios wanted to take a punt on Mrs Brown. He had to beg the Pavilion Theatre to give him a chance, he wouldn't take no for an answer. Unlike in Ireland where he was a household name and a regular on *The Late Late Show*, he was a relative unknown across the water.

He'd tasted some success with the likes of *The Course*, but with no TV and radio exposure and only some local press, he had to rely on word of mouth to build his reputation as the Dublin Ma with the crudest patter.

In June *Mrs Brown's Boys – The Last Wedding* arrived at

the Pavilion Theatre in Glasgow with no reputation, no publicity and initially no sales. But that was to quickly change. Glasgow would fall in love with Mrs Brown; she had found her spiritual home. Just over a decade later she would be filming her first TV series there.

Iain Gordon, the boss at The Pavilion, had initially turned it down. But luckily for him and the future of his theatre, which was struggling financially – and more importantly *Mrs Brown's Boys* – he did a U-turn and she would pull in close to IR£2million at the box office and audiences of 160,000 people.

But when unknown duo Brendan and Gerry first turned up at the theatre, Iain Gordon was prepared to see them off on the first boat back to Ireland. 'The story of how this hit came about in Glasgow is unbelievable,' Iain told the *Evening Times* in 2004. Two Irish guys – complete strangers to me – came to the front door in May four years ago, walked up to the box office and announced "We'd like to hire the Pavilion Theatre for eight weeks. Who do we speak to?"

'My first thought was they must be stupid because Glasgow shuts down in the summer. It's not a busy time for theatre. I was then told the sort of show they had in mind, heard it was an Irish play and figured they were wasting their time.' But they refused to go away.

'All this time I was watching the two guys on CCTV. They just stood there and for some strange reason I felt I could hear their thoughts. And what they were thinking was that there was no way they were going to leave the theatre without seeing me. They didn't.'

Against his better instincts Iain agreed he would read

their script and his first reaction was that thought it was 'awful'.

Brendan and Gerry persuaded him to re-read the script and he also asked actor John Murtagh for a second opinion.

Iain told the *Evening Times*: 'He read it and agreed, "It's not very funny". But an hour later I came back and John stunned me when he began to read the play aloud in an Irish accent. And I started to laugh. And he howled with laughter as well.'

The manager agreed to stage the play, but on opening night of a planned eight-week run, the theatre had only taken IR£5,000 at the box office, hardly enough to cover one night's production.

'I discovered the boys had no money, hoping for good initial returns. But we were facing financial disaster, with an empty theatre for eight weeks. I decided I would pull the show after the first week.'

But on opening night the show was a surprise hit, producing roars of laughter. 'It was the loudest laughter I had ever heard in a theatre. In fact, most of the audience were crying.' The next morning Iain Gordon was laughing as well, all the way to the bank as he saw crowds all the way around the block as he arrived at his theatre.

The audience had gone home and spread the word. 'I reckon we have brought more people back to theatre with *Mrs Brown* than any other company in the past 10 years,' Iain told the *Evening Times*. 'I just wish it had been my idea.'

The Herald (Glasgow) critic wrote that Brendan's performance as Agnes was 'the best drag act since Dame Edna' and 'one of self-absorbed brilliance', while the *Daily Record* said 'There wasn't a dry eye in the house, but all the guests were shedding tears of laughter at the funniest marriage Glasgow has seen in years.'

With Agnes Brown's reputation in Scotland well established, all seemed to be going really well, so it came as a shock, especially to fans, when Brendan's right-hand man Gerry announced that he was quitting the play.

A spokesman told the *Irish Sun* in August 1999: 'Gerry is sick and tired of the road. He has spent 10 years touring and is just worn out.' Gerry was initially set to stay on as Brendan's producer and manager and was said to be upset at being an absent father for his two young kids. 'Gerry and Brendan had a long talk about the shock decision and they will continue to work as business partners. Gerry is just quitting stage work.'

In reality, it was the beginning of the end for the duo, who had been through a lot of stressful projects together, not least *Sparrow's Trap*. At the same time Brendan was making a fist of it with *Mrs Brown's Boys*, and he was still making money from *The Course*, which was enjoying the royalties from a four-month run in Vancouver.

He decided to keep himself in the limelight by taking on any job thrown at him, including a role in August as a judge alongside pop mogul Louis Walsh and Formula One star Eddie Irvine and in the wacky Red Bull Flugtag event at George's Dock Dublin, where folk attempted to launch their own flying machines into the water.

And ever the businessman, Brendan himself had an ambitious idea to launch his own flying machines at the same time – he announced his plans for a IR£75 million new airline called Eir-In linking each of Ireland's airports.

'We have been working on this plan for the past two years and we are very confident that it will be a great success,' he said. Brendan also revealed that as a child his ambition was to be a commercial pilot, but his hopes were dashed in his early teens when he discovered he was colour-blind. A year later he was still adamant it would take off: 'We won't be running airplanes, we'll be running buses with wings,' he quipped. But the crazy plan never got off the ground.

After losing Gerry Browne as an actor, in September that year *Mrs Brown's Boys* lost another cast member when actor Derek Reddin, who played Rory in the play, also quit. It would pave the way for Rory Cowan, Brendan's agent, to try his hand at acting.

Even Derek's farewell party wasn't without drama when thieves tried to make off with Brendan's van, including his props and costumes. Brendan, Derek and friends managed to nab the thieves outside his apartment but the van suffered over IR£1,000-worth of damage.

There was more money hassle when a man who lent IR£10,000 to Brendan for *Sparrow's Trap* went to court in an attempt to get his money back. He wanted a theatre which staged one of Brendan's plays to repay the cash. He asked a judge to order the Everyman Palace Theatre at Cork to give him IR£7,500 from takings.

But barrister John Lucey said the money was owed to the production company which put on *The Last Wedding* and he said it would have a 'calamitous effect' on them if the money was not paid.

Judge A G Murphy asked the Everyman to swear an affidavit that their dealings were with the company and not

Brendan. If they did, he added at Cork Circuit Court, the case could be struck out.

'By the new year everyone will have their money back – I can guarantee that,' Brendan told reporters two days later. 'We'll be out of debt once and for all by then. He lent me IR£10,000 for the film and I appreciate that – I would class him as a friend – and I hope he still is. I can guarantee him he will get his money back.'

And you had to believe him because Brendan has always been a man of integrity, and a man with a huge heart. That Christmas he decided to do his own thing to help the homeless.

He told the *Irish Sun*: 'I invited 25 friends to a party and told them all to bring 25 presents – whether they be pairs of socks or whatever. We then put them all together to make 25 goody bags and everybody had to find a homeless person on the way home and give it to them. I'm going to do it again this year, and it looks like I'll have about 100 people this time.'

His one-man Christmas comedy show ('a history of the 20th Century according to Brendan O'Carroll') titled *Millennium? ...Ask Me Y2K!* featured him as Agnes in part, and got a fair review from *The Sunday Times*:

'Brendan O'Carroll is a benchmark of the new, thrusting Ireland. Is he vulgar and nasty? Is he vulgar and nasty enough? He doesn't have a racist bone in his body, he's just smart enough to know that most of us do.

'He's no more foul-mouthed than has become socially acceptable and no more a misogynist than a frustrated old woman.

'*Ask Me Y2K* showcases O'Carroll at his best and worst.

The feisty Agnes Browne showcases O'Carroll's talent for mimicry and physical comedy and provides him with a persona in which he appears far more comfortable than he does as himself later in the show.'

After a role as one of one of seven presenters for RTE's TV extravaganza, *Millennium Eve - Celebrate 2000*, the new year saw him take *The Course* to Glasgow's Pavilion in February, including his sister Eilish O'Carroll (later to be Winnie in *Mrs Brown's Boys*) and Pat 'Pepsi' Shields (later to be Mark Brown in the show). A glowing review from *The Scotsman* said it provided 'side-splitting laughter'.

Bitten by the movie bug after *Agnes Browne*, Brendan told the *Scottish Daily Mirror* he had plans to take his own version of *Mrs Brown* to the big screen in 2000 with *The Last Wedding*, and decided to Scotland to shoot it in Scotland 'because Irish tax is too high'.

He told the paper: 'The fact is I might have to go to Glasgow to make this movie about a Dublin family and that's a pity. I'd love to be making it here in Ireland.'

Always ambitious, he said he wanted Irish Hollywood stars Gabriel Byrne, Stephen Rea and former *Brookside* actor Bryan Murray, who he worked with on *Sparrow's Trap*, to boost the film's profile.

Brendan said, 'I want them for the Brown family. I would give my right arm to work with Gabriel Byrne. I came very close to working with Stephen Rea before but he was committed to something else. I think those two would be ideal.'

There was more good news for Brendan when the *Irish Sun* reported that his book *The Granny* had clocked up record sales in America. He saw sales of rocket to over 260,000 after a promotional tour of the US.

'We toured 18 cities in 24 days and the response was phenomenal. The book is now number 20 in the bestsellers list there,' he told the *Sun*. 'And the *New York Times* have listed it as one of five books to watch. It's my first time to make the bestsellers' list over there.'

Brendan was also pleasantly shocked when he was given an extra special welcome to the small city of Bethlehem in Pennsylvania – where the City Mayor declared it 'Brendan O'Carroll Day'.

He said: 'They begged me to come there for a signing. They love Mrs Browne for some reason. I've no idea why. So I went along on one of our free days and was blown away by the reception.'

Brendan was welcomed at the city's Moravian Bookstore – one of the oldest in America – by Irish dancers and the City Mayor, with soul singer Gladys Knight providing the entertainment.

City Mayor Donald Cunningham declared August 5 'Brendan O'Carroll Day' because they were so taken with his book *The Mammy*.

Brendan told the *Irish Mirror*: 'I was gobsmacked when I arrived in Bethlehem. It was unbelievable. There were people crying when they met me. I was expecting to walk into a book store and sign a few books and then I heard all this Irish music. When I got to the other side of the store the Mayor was waiting for me.

'There were thousands of people there. I sat signing books until the early hours of the morning. I was really choked about the reception. It was one of my most bizarre experiences.

The Last Wedding headed back to Glasgow in October 2000 and the mutual love affair between Brendan and the city was explored by the *Evening Times* who carried out a voxpop after the show to try and find out why people loved it so much.

Maureen Davies, 34, of Thornliebank, told the paper she was going to see the show for a third time in the same week. 'It's so funny, and she reminds me of my own mum and my gran, who was called Mrs Brown too! I have Irish family roots, and this is just typical of what it's like. I'm bringing along my mum to see it this time, and I'm sure that she will recognise herself in the character.'

And Pat Finnigan, 58, of Castlemilk, was there to see the show for the second time. 'There's nothing to take offence at – it's just a laugh,' she said. 'I don't normally go to the theatre, but my friends told me about this and I came along to have a look. It's some show, it's hilarious.'

The success of his play in Glasgow stunned Brendan, too, he told the *Evening Times*: 'It's been absolutely phenomenal! We add about 10 minutes on to the show when we're here because the audience is laughing so much. Glasgow people have really taken Mrs Brown to their hearts, and I think it's because she reminds some of them of their own mammies.

'Dublin mothers are just like Glasgow ones – fierce and scary, but full of love. She's got a heart of gold and would do anything for her family. I'm so grateful to Glasgow; it really has been the launching pad for us. Before we first came to the city in June 1999, we hadn't made enough money to cover the cost of the production, but it's thanks to the reception we got here that we've gone on to perform in places like New York and Toronto.

'It's incredible really. I walked in here, no one knew me, and told the theatre manager that we'd take in a million for him. He didn't believe us, but now he's had to eat a good slice of humble pie.'

Brendan would barely give himself time to breathe as stand-up was still on the menu back home with a new show called *A Mick In the Kickey* starting a five-night run in Dublin's Olympia Theatre in October, his first stand-up show in over five years.

And Brendan would also take on his first and only panto role in *Treasure Island*, alongside Andy Cameron and Mr Blobby, with Brendan playing the dame Mrs Birdseye. 'She's really a lot like Mrs Brown,' he said. 'Without all the swearing!'

He would swear afterwards never to do panto again, finding it too much of a slog, but it was worthwhile for one reason – he would find friendship and take under his wing a young Gary Hollywood.

He took such a shine to him he created a new character, Dino, for *Mrs Brown's Boys* and even Gary would later admit he had no idea then what an incredible rollercoaster ride he was about to embark on.

CHAPTER 18

MOURNING GLORY

*M*rs *Brown's Boys* was snowballing into a massive success, winning rave reviews and selling out shows across Ireland and the UK. Brendan twigged that this was his chance to build something big; so there was no way he was going to sit on his hands. It wasn't in his character anyway.

By the turn of the new year in 2001 he was already busily writing new material and by February he was putting the finishing touches to his new show, *Good Mourning Mrs Brown,* set to open in Dublin's Gaiety Theatre at the start of April.

The plot for the show centred on Grandad's funeral – except he's not dead. 'Grandad goes to the funeral of one of his friends and gets annoyed that everyone says all these nice things about you after you're dead and you never get to hear them yourself,' explained Brendan.

'So the family decide to hold Grandad's funeral while he's still very much alive. And of course, everything goes haywire after that. It's even funnier than the last one. We're having such a laugh doing it.'

But yet again broadsheet *The Irish Times* was quick to look down its nose at it, and in particular the language employed. 'Most of the time the performance only hinges on the variety of intonations O'Carroll can squeeze out of the F-word,' its critic sneered.

'But this is, after all, just predictable comedy. It's been agreed well in advance of opening night that a typical northside Dublin Mammy swearing like a trooper, joking about vibrators, and wishing Grandad would get his skates on and die is uproariously funny, and it would be foolish to expect anything more comically inventive than this.'

Unable to get their head around the appeal and success of Mrs Brown, *The Irish Times* that same night asked punters why they liked it so much. Anne and Anthony Maher from Kimmage told them they loved 'the Dublin humour' and 'the bad language'.

The Guardian was more generous with its review: 'Brendan O'Carroll's latest big-house comic play sees him triumphantly returning to his variant on the pantomime dame: the sewer-mouthed, chain-smoking Dublin widow Mrs Brown, who rules her extended family with a relentless barrage of one-liners.

'This is really stand-up working-class comedy dressed up as theatre. Just leave your brain at the entrance and let O'Carroll and co deliver the laughs.'

Not so the *Sunday Times* though, who gave it a brutal review, calling it 'a thoroughly depressing comedy where the language may be suitable for adults, but the humour is childish'.

His reputation as comedy's Mr Marmite was already established, with the basic view that working class folk loved him but the middle class loathed him. He was generally feted by the tabloids and often knocked by the broadsheets.

But there was no denying the facts – he was still popular, still selling out shows and everyone had to take notice and appreciate his rise to stardom. And slowly he was winning some critics over, while others could not deny the facts when it came to tickets sales.

Brendan met Gary Hollywood, who plays Rory's boyfriend Dino in the show, when the pair did panto together the previous winter, and signed him up for *Good Mourning Mrs Brown*.

'I came to Glasgow to do the *Treasure Island* panto and that's when I first met Gary,' Brendan told the *Irish Sun*. 'In rehearsals I spotted something special in him. He reminded me a lot of myself. He's a hard worker and always on time, and that's so important when you're staging your own show. The play basically casts itself but after seeing Gary I wrote a new part in for him as Dino, who's Rory's boyfriend.'

Gary jumped at the opportunity. 'I had watched the previous show and I pissed myself laughing. It is the funniest thing I've ever seen on stage. On top of that I got on so well with Brendan so how could I turn him down?

And Gary, who had shot to fame in Scottish soap *High*

Road, found Brendan a kindred spirit, a father figure who helped him nurse his break-up with his fiancée Anne Haney, the mother of his son Zach. Gary had then hit the headlines in Scotland and had been branded a love rat when he started dating panto dancer Sharon Mudie. Brendan, of course, had the experience of his own marriage break-up and was able to lend advice, leading the unlikely duo to forge a strong friendship both on and off-stage.

Gary – who had survived testicular cancer two years previously – told the *Scottish Sun*: 'Brendan really helped me when things went wrong and it ended up in the press. There were so many things said about me that weren't true. But at the end of the day I'm only 22 years old and I made a mistake.

'I've made one mistake in one area of my life, but you learn and someone like Brendan, who knows what he's talking about, helped me through it all. I now call Brendan my adopted dad and I love working with him and his family. When I'm with them I don't have any problems at all.'

'I could help Gary with his problems because I had been through it all myself,' Brendan told the paper. 'I made that announcement on television because I wanted to give my side of the story and not have it distorted.

'The difficult thing is you feel you have let people down with a broken marriage. I'm not just talking about letting your wife down, because that's something you can discuss in private.

'I'm talking about letting down the people in the area I grew up in and who were rooting for me to do well, and then they hear I can't even keep my marriage together

'My marriage is over because my wife wasn't happy and I wasn't happy – thankfully we have three beautiful children and we're still friends, because before we started going out we were mates.'

Brendan's daughter Fiona would also be in the cast of the new play, which included most of the originals from *The Last Wedding*.

It was equally loved again by *The Herald* who called it 'a more extreme version of the *Royle Family* if Lily Savage's Irish auntie moved in as a lodger'. They added, 'If all you want, however, is to relax, sit down and have a laugh, this is priceless entertainment.'

So loved was the show that on 17 June, one fan, lovestruck Frank McGowan, proposed as the stars took their final curtain call. And there were tears, whistles and applause from the 1,500 crowd at the Pavilion Theatre, Glasgow, as blushing Sheila Connolly issued a dramatic 'Yes'.

A sign of his burgeoning success, Brendan was able to buy his Florida holiday home, where he would later celebrate his second marriage with Jenny. The *Orlando Sentinel* reported in October that the Wyndham Palms villa was bought for $187,900.

His irreverent brand of humour was equally loved in Liverpool, and the *Liverpool Echo* reported in their review of *Good Mourning Mrs Brown* at the Royal Court that they were 'even more tempting to review the audience. The smirkers, the smilers, the grinners, the laugh-out-louders and the outright cacklers all add to the welter of fun as feelgood comedy goes into freefall.'

A month later he returned to the city for his Christmas

one-man show – his first English stand-up appearance for five years – called *How's Your Snowballs?*, and in January 2002, talk began of BBC Scotland taking an interest in *Mrs Brown's Boys*.

Brendan is such a tireless worker for charity, there wouldn't be room to list all the events he has supported over the years, but one annual event he would never miss was a celebrity football game every January in aid of Childline and organised by Boyzone's Keith Duffy.

There was a reunion of sorts on the pitch, with Brendan and his old stage partner Gerry Browne turning out together, with Gerry in goal.

Brendan then starred as a guest presenter at the second year of the Meteor Ireland Music Awards in March when Muse, Ronan Keating and The Lighthouse Family all performed at the big bash at the Point Theatre in Dublin where The Cranberries and Westlife and U2 turned up to collect a raft of awards. Pop mogul Simon Cowell also presented an award on the night. Other celebrity presenters include John Hurt and Irish football manager Mick McCarthy.

Meanwhile, Brendan was already writing and planning his next *Mrs Brown's Boys* production.

While in Liverpool to promote a run of *The Course* in May, he told the *Liverpool Echo* that he had plans to stage the world premiere of *Mrs Brown Rides Again* at the Royal Court in a year's time.

The Course, incidentally, went down a storm again and this time his cast was the now mainstay members of *Mrs Brown's Boys*: there were parts for Rory Cowan as the marvellous nervous nerd Tony Short, Paddy Houlihan as the country lad Ben Wilson, Pat Shields as the frustrated actor Bill Weston, Fiona O'Carroll as the luscious Tina and, of course, Jennifer Gibney as the staid Emily.

Success on different fronts has been a great business model for Brendan, who after *Mrs Brown's Boys* took *The Course* on tour again and saw his book *The Mammy* published in another new market, this time Australia.

Critics greeted it generally enthusiastically. The *Hobart Mercury* said, 'This magic read is far from depressing. The tears that fall on the pages are from laughter, rather than sadness.'

And the *Canberra Times* reported: 'Brendan O'Carroll's books have taken eight years to come to Australia, a delay caused mainly by negotiations with publishers they were originally published by a house specialising in school textbooks.

'In that time, *The Mammy* has been translated into half a dozen languages and filmed under the title *Agnes Browne* with Anjelica Huston in the title role.

'These are warm, feel-good stories – keep a box of tissues handy – that show how simple Dublin goodness can cope with waywardness, bossy officialdom or sinister evil.

'Brendan O'Carroll is better known as a stand-up comedian and television performer, but he does not overdo the comedy or let it interfere with his storyline, and indeed he appeals more to the tear ducts than the funny bone.'

And in a bid to cash in on his success further, if not prompt a TV series, Brendan and his company Brendan O'Carroll Productions took *Mrs Brown* into the video market.

'RTE have given us IR£20,000 to develop it for a new

series,' he told the *Irish Sun*. 'The new head of entertainment came and saw me and offered it. Basically, what I'm going to do is put pictures to the original *Mrs Browne's Boys* radio show we had on 2FM back in 1992. There will be six in the first series.' The videos featured cameos by ex-Boyzone stars Ronan Keating and Keith Duffy and Gay Byrne – who gave him his very first break on *The Late Late Show*.

He also created parts for his children in the videos, and on stage, telling the *Irish Sunday Mirror*: 'My kids grew up in the entertainment business so it was kind of obvious that they were all going to follow me into it. Fiona [then 22] was the first to come on board. She was actually a hit before I was. When she was only nine-years-old she went to No 6 in the Irish charts with a song called Christmas Rapper.

'In the past she was always saying how she wanted to work with me but I felt she was just that little bit too young. But then when the part of Maria came up in the second Mrs Brown play I offered it to her as I felt she was ready. And when I came up with the part of Trevor, Danny had left school and was getting ready to do acting lessons.

'We came to an agreement that he could have the part as long as he takes technique lessons when we're off the road. So we're together all the time and in that respect we're really lucky – we're like the Partridge Family.'

Although Brendan's youngest child Eric – who was 10 at the time – was still a bit young to join in the touring production, he appeared in the video as Mrs Brown's grandson, Bono.

'Even though he's only 10, Eric is already a sucker for the business. He's been in *Angela's Ashes* and countless student movies and now he's in *Mrs Brown's Boys* as well. I'm 47, and in my house I feel like an under-achiever.'

Brendan told the paper he had no qualms about Eric being exposed to the bad language and racy plots of his work: 'The way I look at it is anything in the show that they understand, they are old enough to understand it. And anything they don't, well, it'll do no harm as it just goes over their heads. They are well able to look after themselves – they have been hand-reared and I have no worries about them.'

Brendan had early – and high – hopes that after seeing the first video it would get commissioned for a TV series.

'I think it would make a good television series,' he said. 'If it works in every other medium like books, video and in the theatre, why not television?'

The *Mrs Brown's Boys* video was a hit with the public, outstripping the combined sales of both *Spiderman* and popular Irish TV comedy impressions show *Aprés Match* in Ireland. The relentlessly busy Brendan made the videos and was ready the next month to take Mrs Brown on the road again with new show *Mrs Brown Rides Again*.

After that, he already had plans to head off to America again to promote a new book, *The Young Wan*, the prequel to his Agnes Browne trilogy, and meanwhile on the home front, Brendan and Jenny bought their first house together as their relationship started to really blossom. 'Life is good and if it gets any better than this then I'm getting someone else's share of happiness.'

Brendan knows all too painfully the heartache of losing a child. He didn't get long with baby Brendan, so he could only imagine how hard it was for his friend Mike Nolan, whose nine-year-old daughter Grace died from a rare blood disorder on 10 November 1999.

Mike set up a charity in her memory, the Grace Nolan Foundation, with Brendan as a trustee, which published a book, Dear Grace, with contributions by schoolchildren, to raise funds. 'The book is very important because children all over the country participated in it,' Mike told the *Irish Daily Mirror*.

'We ran a nationwide short story competition during the year and the winners had their pieces made into the book. The kids wrote to Grace as if she was their penpal and they told her all about what happened during the year.

'But for me the most touching bits of the book are the messages from Grace's schoolmates. I never knew of the kids' pain and reading their letters I realise what they went through also. We love and miss Grace deeply and her short life is my inspiration, to continue this work in her honour especially to prevent the tragic loss of a child to HHT wherever they are in the world.'

CHAPTER 19

BRENDAN FOR PRESIDENT!

Inside Brendan O'Carroll there is a burning ambition: a passion to be a politician radiates within his very bones. It's in his DNA, borne from his love and admiration for his mother Maureen, Ireland's first female parliamentarian.

And as we know by now, Brendan's not one to settle for second best. He wouldn't simply be happy to be a TD like his mum. He believes anything is possible and can even see himself as President or Taoiseach – the Irish Prime Minister – one day.

He told the *Irish Sunday Mirror* in November 2005 of his desire to move into politics, and was clear that he's not having a laugh, although he shares a common view with the man in the street that Irish politics is a joke.

'It's time for a brand new political party in Ireland,' he

told the paper. 'There needs to be a meeting of minds with mine on a new political party, like a Social Justice party; one that would come to the table with clean hands. Not with a history of violence behind them, a history of civil war nor a history of taking brown envelopes.

'What is needed are sharp-minded business people and community leaders who are interested only in furthering the challenges we are meeting in Ireland.'

Brendan, whose mum was a Labour TD for Dublin North Central, says his new party would be 'left-centre'. He is a big supporter of the European Union and believes immigration is a big issue for both Ireland and its immigrants.

And the Government's ad hoc solutions for immigration won't wash with Brendan. He said long theatre tours would be out if he moved into politics, but the bright lights of the stage would be too much to give up altogether.

'I don't think I could completely say goodbye to my career,' he mused to the *Irish Sunday Mirror*. 'I would have to curtail my activities. I am not fully financially in a position to say I don't need the money.'

He reiterated his plans to the respected Irish broadsheet *The Sunday Independent*. The Celtic Tiger has created such social chaos, he argued, that as an island nation, 'we should never privatise our national airline and other infrastructure'.

His plans have been long-held. In 1999 he declared he remained 'deadly serious' about his oft-expressed ambition to follow in his mother's footsteps and stand as an independent socialist TD in Finglas, where he grew up. In 2003 he told the *Irish News of the World* he was on the brink of standing for election then, and had been courted across the political divide in Ireland.

'I will run for office. I would say it will probably be at the next election. I've been approached by all the main parties, but I probably wouldn't run for Labour. At the moment I have a few consultants drawing up a manifesto for a new party.'

There's no doubting his pedigree, considering the political achievements of his mother and his membership of Mensa with an IQ of 153 and he has said that said that anyone who thinks he's a joker and unable to cut it as a politico will be found wanting.

'Anyone who underestimates me is a very silly person,' he told the *Sunday Business Post*. 'I am not a gobshite. I've worked my way up from nothing. I'm a member of Mensa. I've made a career in comedy, the hardest profession in the world. And when I become a TD and start changing the political culture of this country, a lot of people are going to have to revise their opinion of Brendan O'Carroll.'

Perhaps if it had not been for the phenomenal success of *Mrs Brown's Boys* once it went to television he might have stood already.

He told the *Irish Examiner* in February 2009 that he was mulling over whether to run in the next General Election. The prospect of a Labour Taoiseach had prompted him to consider running on the party ticket in the next election in 2012. He is a member of the party.

'I have always been interested in running but not until such time as the Labour Party would be in a position to produce a Labour Taoiseach,' he said. He also said enhancing infrastructure and getting the country back to work would be his two biggest priorities if he were to run.

Brendan said in May the same year that it was the fallout from the recession that was awakening his political wanderlust.

He told the *Irish Sun*: 'We can get out of the recession, but it's about all of us. Either we all go forward together or we'll all go backwards. We need to be led. Brian Cowen, I think, can do it. But I just don't know why he isn't. He should call me and say, "Brendan, this is the message, how do I say it?" Because I'd be great at doing that for him.'

And Brendan reckons he knows how to make everything right. He insisted: 'The best thing to put smiles on people's faces is enough money to live. That's all people want. I don't care how funny you think you are, if you've got somebody who's under pressure for money then they won't laugh.

'I have ideas but the things that I'd want to bring in would probably be illegal and you wouldn't want to hear them. All I can say is "spend, spend, spend, borrow like fuck". Spend every penny you can get your hands on.'

His political aspirations would not leave him. He told the *Irish Sun* again in September 2011 he was edging closer to making a move as a TD. Brendan, then 55, insisted his policies will be about the good of the country rather than popularity. He explained: 'It's not something I could have done last year or four years ago but it's something I hope to be able to do soon. I laid down conditions a number of years ago that I said I'd achieve before running.

'One was that I wouldn't need the money and the other was that I'd be in a position to do something. I can see those conditions coming about by the next election. If you're dependant on getting re-elected because you need the income, a lot of your decisions are about keeping people happy. I'd prefer to be in a position where I could do things because they're right.' He spoke again of his plans to establish his own Social Justice Party. And he told how he'd like to see Ireland make an economic recovery by implementing a flat rate tax of 20 per cent.

In March 2012 he told the Irish magazine *RSVP* that he was hoping to field an entire political party in the General Election. The magazine said he had already registered the Social Justice Party and Brendan had plans for Ryanair boss Michael O'Leary to become a TD with him.

'I'd like to pick 12 people whom I feel could make a difference but right now I think it's time to consolidate and look after my family,' he told *RSVP*. 'I feel that Michael O'Leary makes a lot of sense in the things he says. I would have had Eamon Coughlan as one of the 12, but he's joined Fine Gael.'

Brendan told the magazine he feels depressed whenever he comes home to Ireland from his base in Florida – and believes America is tackling the recession better than here. And he blasted the Government for failing to help people on the poverty line.

He added: 'You feel depression as soon as you arrive back. The US has the spirit of trying to keep going through it all. Last Christmas, they closed Disneyland as the parks were all booked out - despite the recession.

'In Ireland I hear that savings have gone up by 6% to 8%. People are afraid to spend. I think you'd want a cup of arsenic if you listened to Morning Ireland every day. It can be terribly depressing.'

He told Highland Radio in May 2012 he was edging

closer to the world of politics and had not ruled out running for a seat in the Dáil, adding that he would only ever run for the Dáil if he could manage to not be reliant on a TD's salary.

'I always said that I wouldn't run until such time as I didn't need the money. I didn't want to be in a position where I needed to stay elected to get the money, because I don't think your thinking would be the same.

'I'm getting closer and closer to that stage… I'd love to serve my country, love to.'

CHAPTER 20

TICKET TO RIDE

By 2003 *Mrs Brown's Boys'* reputation was continuing to grow and Brendan wanted to keep it mushrooming by quickly rolling out another hit play.

His new show, *Mrs Brown Rides Again*, meant that he could now boast a trilogy and as this was the third instalment, it would be easy to promote, as eager fans would clamour for tickets to what they thought would be the last helping of the dysfunctional Brown family headed by Agnes, the fag-smoking, cider-voiced Dublin matriarch with a laugh like a rattlesnake.

The plot this time would centre on Agnes overhearing her kids talking about plans to put the ailing family dog Spartacus in a home. Agnes thinks they are talking about her and to prove her children wrong she displays a new lease of life.

Brendan took the show to Dublin's Olympia Theatre for its premiere and an unprecedented 31 shows. And it looked as if Brendan was winning over *The Irish Times*, whose critic wrote: 'A packed Olympia again rocked with laughter this week at the further antics of his belligerent, quick-witted and contemptuous auld wan. On my way out I heard nothing but praise: "Ah, it was a great roar" ... "It was a brilliant laugh". And I'm not going to argue with that.'

In his programme notes Brendan mentions a teacher, Mr Muldoon, who told him when he was 10 that he would always be a loser. His defiant reply? 'If by any chance you are still alive and here tonight, Mr Muldoon... ask me bollox!'

Ireland boss Brian Kerr even took his entire football squad to The Olympia to see the show and boost team morale.

Straight after his run at the Olympia, Brendan flew to the US in February to promote his latest book, *The Young Wan*, while in Glasgow, theatre box office records were being smashed as people clamoured for tickets for the new *Mrs Brown* play in Glasgow by the start of March, five weeks before the show was due to open. More than 19,000 tickets were sold for the show at the Pavilion Theatre, making it their fastest and biggest-selling play to date.

Brendan's home from home, Glasgow, was glad to see him back, and he told the *Daily Record*: 'People identify with her,' he said. 'Initially, I thought Mrs Brown was an intrinsically Dublin woman with an intrinsically Dublin story, but I get letters from Bombay to Brooklyn telling me that they know this woman.

'She reminds people of their granny or their mother. There is a touch of nostalgia in it, too. I think that's why people find it so appealing.'

Inevitably though, there is one snag he associates with the role, as he told the paper: 'There can be few things worse than wearing a pair of mesh tights cutting the crotch off you. I don't know how they wear them. I wouldn't be a woman for all the tea in China.

'But people don't ever see me here without my Mrs Brown wig and frock on. And I'm getting really expert at dressing up in women's clothes. I can put my lipstick on in two seconds flat.'

When the show went to Liverpool, the *Liverpool Echo* reported how his Royal Court show helped raise IR£2,500 for the Red Cross after Brendan asked audiences to contribute at the end of each show. Brendan was also a continued supporter of showbiz pal Keith Duffy's fundraising campaigns for autism charities – his daughter Mia is autistic – including dinners and celebrity golf tournaments.

He would almost always appear as himself at such events, but he broke with convention to appear as Agnes that Christmas for the Grace Nolan Foundation. Brendan organised a Mrs Brown's Christmas Party – a €1,500-a-table Christmas dinner with a difference, as Irish celebrities serving up the grub included RTE radio host Joe Duffy, actress Twink (Adele King) and Boyzone and *Coronation Street* star Keith Duffy. Brendan also had a role for Joe Duffy in his second DVD, *Mrs Brown's Boys Part Two*, as well as MEP Proinsias DeRossa and former athlete Eamon Coughlan.

Every year Brendan retires to his Florida holiday home to recharge his batteries – and little wonder given the phenomenal workload he takes on year after year, and not just writing new instalments of the *Mrs Brown's Boys* plays.

He would simultaneously be planning to roll out Mrs Brown and her brood to new markets, cities he hadn't taken her to before.

By this stage Brendan was already officially established as the most successful Irish comedian ever. Since *The Last Wedding* first opened in 1999 it had broken box office records all over Ireland and the UK.

In the Pavilion Theatre, Glasgow, the play had grossed over one and a half million pounds at the box office in five years, making it the most successful show ever there. In the Royal Court Theatre in Liverpool it broke the box office record, previously held by Paul McCartney. In Dublin the manager of the Gaiety said that Brendan is the only Irish playwright that is capable of playing for 12 sold-out weeks in his theatre.

And in April 2004 he made first forays to the likes of Birmingham and Newcastle with his first play in the series. Brendan's plan was then to hit them with the next two plays within a year. He told Birmingham's *Evening Mail*: 'I could say I had this master plan where I came up with this brilliant idea, but the truth is I didn't have a clue at all. It's been absolutely amazing, just astounding. Mrs Brown has been translated into 17 languages and has been No 1 in places like China and Bosnia.

'I think people of all nationalities and religions will recognise this woman, so much so that I get letters from Bombay to the Bronx saying they have a Mrs Brown living down their street. She's a collaboration of those tough old women who can break walnuts in their teeth but wouldn't have a bad word to say about their children.'

But the character's success at this time forced Brendan to make a hard decision.

'I have to put a rein on it because there are other projects I want to do, and I don't want to get bogged down with it, so I'm restricting *Mrs Brown* to 26 weeks a year,' he revealed. This was telling – Brendan had made an important life decision, from which he would resolutely refuse to budge. From now on, he said, he would work 26 weeks and rest 26 weeks.

Brendan makes no apologies for the colourful language in the *Mrs Brown* plays, something that would come back time and again as an issue amongst critics and punters, especially when they later moved to television.

One letter, from K Burgess of Pelsall, in Birmingham's *Evening Mail* was typical: 'I am writing to warn your readers that the language in *Mrs Brown's Last Wedding*, at the Alexandra Theatre, is shocking. But this is not a complaint. Brendan O'Carroll is quite brilliant as Mrs Agnes Brown and the show is two hours of great Irish humour. I haven't laughed so much since Tony Blair said "Trust me".'

When *Mrs Brown* opened at Newcastle's Opera House the *Evening Chronicle* hailed it as a triumph: 'Lifting the typical Irish mammy out of the living room, with mannerisms and foul language to boot, in an ingenious display of comic writing, stand-up comedian Brendan O'Carroll thrilled the eager, opening night crowd, with his no holds barred exposé of the manipulations and humour behind the closed doors of a Dublin household.

'O'Carroll most definitely has a sinful way with words and can ad-lib for Ireland, which shows why he is top of his game, and so loved in his homeland. The supporting cast of 11 blatantly enjoyed every moment, finding themselves holding back cries of laughter and forgetting lines in the process. They gave a cracker of a performance, regardless.'

The same year Brendan told of only discovering that he was dyslexic. 'I only realised when I brought my youngest child Eric for a test,' he said. 'Eric, Danny and I are all dyslexic – we have problems reading from left to right which makes our reading speed slower.'

It makes the fact that he is one of the elite few members (around 1,200 in Ireland) of the high IQ society Mensa all the more impressive. Speed of thought wasn't a problem for Brendan when he did the Mensa supervised test many years ago.

'I had to leave early to collect my daughter Fiona from Irish dancing class, so I flew through the answers and was convinced I hadn't a chance. When I got the letter, I was shocked,' he told the *Irish Independent* that July.

'As my mother used to say, never confuse education with intelligence,' said Brendan, who left school at 12 and was still waiting tables when he joined Mensa. I love books, but I'm a slow reader. In fact, I have the reading speed of a 12-year-old. My sons, Danny and Eric, are also dyslexic.

'I'll never forget the day Danny was waiting for his results and he said, "I hope I have dyslexia and I'm not just thick." I assured him that he wasn't thick. Einstein, Sir Francis Bacon and lots of other well-known figures had dyslexia.

'Now if I meet a bunch of children in the Dyslexia Association, I'll produce my gold card from Mensa and say, "Look, only the top two per cent in the world get this – and I'm dyslexic." I want them to know what they're capable of.'

Brendan and son Eric, who was 12 at the time, were

interviewed for the *Sunday Independent* that October to promote a fundraiser for special teaching for disadvantaged children with dyslexia.

'I didn't even know what they were talking about,' Brendan said of the moment he was told Eric could be dyslexic. 'They said he'd need resource teaching and maybe some extra teaching outside school and I was nodding away and then the expert said, "You know dyslexia usually runs through the male line of the family?"

'It didn't click for a minute, I thought, "God, how stupid was my da?"' Brendan was given a page to read and told he had the reading speed of a 12-year-old. 'I always knew I read slowly, but I thought it was because I was really concentrating. I told her I'd written four novels, six screenplays and four plays and she told me that William Butler Yeats was dyslexic.'

'And Leonardo da Vinci and Einstein,' Eric piped up during the *Sunday Independent* interview.

'My kids are very lucky,' added Brendan, 'because they're not afraid. For my kids, finding out they have dyslexia hasn't been a scary thing, it has been like a light coming on. It made so many things make sense.'

With Fiona and Danny already joining their dad in *Mrs Brown's Boys*, Eric enthusiastically declared 'me next'. For the last two years, Eric had played Bono, Mrs Brown's grandson, in his father's videos and was itching to join the stage show too.

Around the same time, Brendan would finally get his first break on British TV – thanks to his friend Peter Kay, who gave him a cameo in *Max and Paddy's Road to Nowhere*, the spin-off from sitcom *Phoenix Nights*.

Comedian Paddy McGuinness, who plays one half of the hapless bouncer duo with his best pal Peter Kay, said they first met Brendan on the comedy circuit in Manchester.

Brendan told the *Irish Sun* that a chance meeting with Kay at a charity event saw him win the part: 'We met briefly at a function for Keith Duffy's autism charity in Dublin. Peter told me he was doing a spin-off series of *Phoenix Nights* and asked if I would like to play a role. I didn't need asking twice.'

He even did his own stunts – including a 20-ft plunge – despite being offered a stuntman.

He said, 'I told them I'd rather do it myself than be standing around. I did it 16 times. I think that by the end of it, I was a fully fledged paratrooper!'

In October, Brendan was taking *Good Mourning Mrs Brown* on tour again to the likes of Glasgow, Birmingham and Newcastle. The reputation was growing, the crowds were flocking and the local press were still lapping it up too.

The *Newcastle Evening Chronicle* called it 'a cross between *Father Ted* and *The Royle Family*' and 'without a doubt the greatest display of comedy theatre' they had seen all year.

Mrs Brown had a number of celebrity fans even before the TV show and Brendan enjoyed giving them cameos either on stage or in the DVDs he produced with his own company, BOC Productions.

Footballer Robbie Keane, who played with the likes of Liverpool and Tottenham Hotspur, and former world snooker champion Ken Doherty would appearing in his next DVD – as Mormons.

And the pair found it so hilarious they took a full day to film their two-minute doorstep scene.

The new DVD was called *Mrs Brown's Boys – Believe It Or Not*, and was the third in the series.

Brendan revealed that LA Galaxy striker Robbie Keane is such a big fan of the character that he often puts on her voice in phone calls. He told the *Irish Sun*: 'Ken Doherty was going to appear in the last DVD and I had a scene written for him where Agnes confuses him for a waiter when he's walking through a hotel in his waistcoat on the way to a snooker tournament.

'But his schedule got too busy and he couldn't do it. Ken then asked for a role in the new one, but I didn't know what to give him. Then Robbie Keane – who is a huge Mrs Brown fan – rang up looking for a small part as well. So I made the two of them Mormons who call to Mrs Brown's front door to convert her.

'Robbie often rings up and leaves me messages on the answer phone in a Mrs Brown voice. He loves it. In fact most of the Ireland soccer squad are fans.'

And *Coronation Street* star Keith Duffy also appeared as a garda, Slick Mick, in a love interest for Cathy.

By this stage, the ever-ambitious Brendan had built his own studio set and offices in Blanchardstown, and said he was planning to make at least 10 *Mrs Brown* DVDs. The DVD would go down well back home, third in the official Irish video and DVD charts for Christmas week after Pat Shortt's *Killinaskully*, a popular RTE comedy TV series, and a Tommy Tiernan live stand-up performance.

The reputation and appeal of *Mrs Brown's Boys* was growing apace.

CHAPTER 21

MAKING AN HONEST WOMAN OF JENNY

It dawned on Brendan – more than six years after he announced his marriage was over and he was spotted stepping out with Jenny Gibney – that after falling madly in love with her, he finally had to make an honest woman of her.

Although, it wasn't the most romantic setting when he had his epiphany.

He revealed to the *Irish Sun* in 2007: 'I remember coming down at five in the morning and turning on the television. Sky News was on and I lit up a cigarette. Suddenly I thought to myself, "Hang on, I'm 48 and what would I do if I woke up tomorrow and Jenny wasn't there?" I made up my mind then and there to marry her.'

The pair had discovered they were soulmates and had no

problems working and living together and Brendan has said Jenny was 'one in a million'. They had already been through enough ups and downs to know they could stick together through thick and thin.

'There was a time when none of us had any money and we didn't know which way to turn,' he says. 'She went out and borrowed money on her credit card to keep us going.'

The pair would get the legal side things cemented at a registry office in Dublin on 1 August 2005. And the next month the pair tied the knot in style with a ceremony in his beloved Florida. 'It feels fantastic being married,' said Brendan afterwards.' We've been living together for a long time so it's nice to know that she's legally entitled to be there.'

Des Willoughby, the popular tenor, sang at the wedding party, including a rendition of *You Raise Me Up*. 'Brendan's wife Jenny loved that song and wanted it played as she walked up the aisle with her father,' Des told the *Wicklow People* later. 'As a surprise, Brendan flew me out to Florida and hid me from Jenny until the morning of the wedding. It was great to see the happy surprise on her face when she saw me standing there singing. It was the best wedding I've ever been to. Brendan's been very good to me over the years and I do a lot of his charity events.'

Brendan told his pal Gay Byrne that the deal with the hotel for the reception, for food and drink for all the guests was $10,000.

'Brendan thought it was very reasonable indeed,' Gay told the *Sunday Independent*. 'And on the day, everything was perfect and they all folded up about 3am and everyone delighted with themselves.

'The next morning, Brendan got a call from the catering

manager to say that the food and drink consumed at the reception was rather less than they'd catered for, and that therefore Brendan was due a refund of $2,500! Dear sweet Mother of Divine Grace, when would this ever happen in Ireland!'

A year into his marriage Brendan revealed to the *Irish Sunday Mirror* that, even though by now he had become a grandfather, he was also considering becoming a father again and have a child with Jenny. 'We haven't ruled it out, we're talking about it.' he said. 'My son Danny just became a father, his wife had a son, little Jamie. And my daughter Fiona is due a baby in March so I'm going to be a double grandad. So if we have a child it will have three little kids to play with if you count the father.'

CHAPTER 22

FEELING THE LOVE

By March 2005, Brendan was milking every last pound from *Mrs Brown's Boys*, with the third part of the trilogy packing them out everywhere.

Yet again he had smashed theatre box-office records in Glasgow after selling half-a-million tickets in a single theatre – pulling in IR£5million for the once-troubled Pavilion Theatre. Yes, Brendan had become the most successful comedian Ireland has ever produced, but he was quick to pay tribute to those who paved the way before him, such as Dave Allen who died aged 68 on 11 March 2005.

'Dave was one of the best comedians I ever saw,' said Brendan. 'He changed the way Irish people think about themselves. He will never be forgotten.'

When his show hit Newcastle's Journal Tyne Theatre in June, Peter Kay and his mates were there to see it. And Kay went one better when it played Manchester that October when he jumped on stage in a flat cap and boiler suit for a cameo appearance. He even put on an Irish accent for his mate Brendan, which was easy for him as he grew up mimicking his mum, who is from Co Tyrone.

With such continued success Brendan, by now living with Jenny in Hollystown in north Dublin, was laughing all the way to the bank – and the press were noseying into Brendan's business accounts.

The *Irish Independent* reported in October 2005 that the most recent accounts for his companies showed they had mixed fortunes in 2003, with one firm making a profit of over €250,000.

'One company, Mrs Browne's Boys Ltd, had accumulated profits of €416,252 by the end of 2003, up from €152,000 in 2002. This indicates an impressive profit of €263,000 in 2003. Another company owned by O'Carroll, BOC Productions Ltd, had accumulated losses of €318,987 by the end of February 2004. This was up from €183,559 a year earlier, indicating an after-tax loss of €135,000 in 2003/2004.'

He decided to take a break from Mrs Brown that November with his first stand-up show for six years – *How's Your Wibbly Wobbly Wonder*. It would be a rare run of performances of his once outrageously blue stand-up act, first at Dublin's Olympia and then heading across the Irish Sea to the Glasgow and other cities.

He told the *Irish Sun* the reason why he felt like flying solo for a change: 'I'm a star in Britain but very few people even know what I look like,' he explained. 'They've fallen for Mrs Brown, not Brendan O'Carroll. They've no idea who he is.

'I've never even done my stand-up act over there. I now love nothing better than going backstage after the show, taking off the gear and slipping down to the theatre bar. I eavesdrop there on what people thought of the show. And sometimes they draw me into conversations about Mrs Brown – and they haven't a clue who I am. It's very entertaining and very insightful for me. I love it. It gives me a real kick.

'The success in the UK has really blown me away. It started off in Scotland and then spread down south. But we've put a lot of work into it, it didn't come easy. I now spend more time over there than I do here.'

With three hit plays under his belt, Brendan hit on his next money-making idea in September 2006 – run the trilogy back-to-back spread over an incredible six weeks in a row. And where else, but his second home Glasgow.

Gary Hollywood – Dino in *Mrs Brown's Boys* – said that by this stage he had come to realise that Brendan was like no other employer. 'He's entirely protective of everyone around him,' he told the *Evening Times*. 'If you have a problem Brendan senses that and tries to sort it. He can read people so well. He's an incredibly caring man.

'Most of the cast of Mrs Brown are friends and family and what happens is you become part of that extended family. You know, I have to say I would trust him with my life.'

At Brendan's Hollystown home, a luxury development with a golf course almost in the backyard, the bright decor indicates a fun home, the walls plastered with photos of Brendan's three kids and second wife, Jenny. Not far away are the offices of BOC Productions, a purpose-built building revealing not only is he a writer but the boss of a major production company which by that stage was making Mrs Brown videos, creating the sets for the shows and covers every aspect of merchandising them.

'I'm a Heinz 57 man,' he says, borrowing a nickname his mum used to give him. 'I do all sorts.' That would certainly always be the case with Brendan, a tireless worker and creative force. But he believed Mrs Brown wasn't a success just because she's funny, but because she leads us towards the light. 'She does,' says Brendan. 'She has a basic sense of what's right.'

So too does Brendan, a man who combines artistic talent with a sharp business mind. He has developed a property portfolio, buying two apartments in Shanghai, and his kids Fiona and Danny own homes in the same street in Florida where he lives for half the year.

Brendan's a livewire, the original man who can't sit still, so retiring to his Florida holiday home each year isn't simply to relax. Often he'll work, write new material, but he's a social animal and loves to have the company of family around him as well as inviting a host of friends year after year.

And each year Brendan and his celebrity friends compete in his annual golf tournament at the Crooked Cat course in Orlando, where the winner gets awarded the 'Crystal Mickey'.

The fourth part of the Mrs Brown trilogy – *For The Love of Mrs Brown* launched in Glasgow at the end of

February, at the old favourite The Pavilion with a month of shows booked throughout the March.

One of the gags in the new play involved comments that Mrs Brown may be a little overweight: 'She has a suit upstairs she can't get into and she wants to fit it in time for Valentine's Day. Her daughter tells her that the only way to get a date at short notice is on the internet. She finds three men, one of them known as Hairy Harry. The consequences are hilarious.'

There were subplots featuring gay son Rory's failing romance, and daughter Cathy's decision to have plastic surgery and the exchange: 'Mammy, I'm going to have a boob job.' 'Why, what's the matter with the job you've got?' And Grandad has discovered a cure for erectile dysfunction and Mrs Brown takes LSD.

The new show was another massive hit, but rather than roll it out around the country right away, Brendan wanted to whet the appetite elsewhere and milk his other shows first. In April he took *Mrs Brown Rides Again* to the Alexandra Theatre, Birmingham, before heading to Dublin to do the trilogy back-to-back, billed as *The Mrs Brown Festival*.

But there was real drama later that month when Brendan told the *Irish Sun* how the infamous Friday the 13th was almost a very black day for him. He felt his world was ending when daughter Fiona was forced to have an emergency C-section because her unborn-baby's heart had stopped.

It brought back horrific memories of the problematic births if his first and last children, Brendan who passed away days after being born and Eric who was lucky to survive. And his first wife Doreen was lucky to survive herself on both occasions.

This time he was even more stressed out, not just because it was his darling daughter but also because on the same day he heard his father-in-law, Michael, had been found unconscious in his back garden after collapsing and had been rushed to hospital. To make matters worse, the star, then 50, was hundreds of miles away in Birmingham on his Mrs Brown tour of the UK.

But the day was to end happily. He received a call saying that doctors knew what was wrong with Michael and a small procedure would change his life. And half an hour after that he got a text saying: 'Baby Felix born, seven pounds, everybody fine'.

'Talk about a day flipping over from a nightmare situation to a dream come true.'

That Christmas, Brendan made an annual pilgrimage to his own slice of heaven, his Miami holiday home hideaway. The area is favoured by several of Ireland's rich and famous – Boyzone's Keith Duffy, comedian Brendan Grace, singer Red Hurley and X Factor judge Louis Walsh all have places there.

He flew out out with wife Jenny on Boxing Day, or St Stephen's Day as it is called in Ireland, to recharge the batteries before his first tour of new play *For The Love Of Mrs Brown*. When the show – 'the fourth part in the trilogy' – opened to packed audiences in January 2008 one pundit was quoted as saying it was funnier than all previous three put together. Brendan too thought it was his best piece of work to date.

'When I sat down to write *For the Love of Mrs Brown*, I was terrified. I thought, "What am I doing?" he told the *Newcastle Evening Chronicle*. 'The other three were so successful, so I hoped to try and get something that was as good so it could stand up with the other three.

'I swear, this has turned out to be the funniest thing I have ever written, not just the funniest *Mrs Brown*. I'm bursting my heart laughing – and I know what's coming next. I find writing very relaxing. As my mother used to say, "If you are doing something you love, you'll never work a day in your life."'

Brendan told the *Evening Chronicle* why he though Mrs Brown was so loved in the region: 'As far as the North East is concerned, this could be Dublin, this could be Ireland. The wit, the speed of it, they are so far ahead of you. They are so far ahead of any other audience – they are getting punchlines before you even get to them.

'Someone told me the reason for that is because when the lights come up, the Newcastle audiences go "we know her, this woman is a local". She's exactly like the mothers and the grannies they knew from the past.

'A lot of it has gone – the collieries have gone, the shipbuilding is gone, and with them a lot of those old characters, the old grannies, the settlements, communities. They say boys turn into their fathers and girls turn into their mothers – in my case I think I'm turning into my mother!

'I didn't have a dad, he died when I was very young, so my only perspective in life was from a female perspective, which is a great help for Agnes.'

When the show arrived in Dublin at the end of the month the audience for its Irish premiere was packed with showbiz pals – comic Peter Kay, former Miss World Rosanna Davison, boxer Bernard Dunne and Keith Duffy.

Meanwhile in February the Irish Film Board released a list of the biggest home-grown movies of the decade – *Agnes Browne* came in eighth place with €700,000 in box office sales. Not quite the flop many would have had you believe after all.

That same month Brendan told Liverpool's *Daily Post* more about the writing process for *Mrs Brown's Boys*, with Brendan always preferring to work through the night to craft his comedy. Each morning, his wife, Jenny – Cathy Brown in all the shows – takes a look at what he has done.

'But she is my wife and she loves me so when she tells me it is brilliant you don't know whether it is or she is just delighted that you're writing,' said Brendan. 'Once the script is completed, I get all the cast together for the first read through and watch them to see if they laugh.

'You see, they know the characters inside out and if they do laugh that is OK. But then you get to rehearsals and when you rehearse it and rehearse again it's like hearing the same joke over and over again. It's funny when you first hear it, but after 10 times you are pleading not to be told that joke again.'

By opening night, he says, he is standing in the wings asking himself again if the show is funny.

'You know as soon as you hit the lights and get that first laugh. Then you kid yourself and say you knew that would get a laugh. You lying devil.'

Brendan claimed that the new show was 'not just the

funniest *Mrs Brown* but the funniest thing I have ever written. I just thank the comedy gods because I don't know where it came from.'

Mrs Brown herself, incidentally is reckoned to be aged around 66. 'I think she's 74 but if you ask her she's 66,' says Brendan.

He introduced Mrs Brown to British audiences at Liverpool's Royal Court Theatre some years back and it quickly became home to his biggest fan base in England.

'They took a flyer on me and I took a flyer on them,' he told the *Liverpool Daily Post*. 'We did three weeks there and it just became an amazing success for us. I kind of feel that, although Mrs Brown is based in Dublin, her spiritual home is Liverpool.

'In the early days, it was Mrs Who? But Liverpool audiences stuck with us through and through, so when I heard Liverpool was going to be European Capital of Culture, I wanted to be part of it.

'I get letters from Bombay, Hawaii, Tokyo, everywhere and they all say Mrs Brown is like their granny or mother-in-law. She's universal. I get people in Bristol telling me she lives just down the road.'

The two years O'Carroll spent thinking of the new Mrs Brown play were useful, he said, dreaming up a whole series of different scenes, but it would be by no means his last. Brendan told the *Birmingham Mail* that he could see no end to the *Mrs Brown's Boys* plays – as long as the demand was still there.

'As soon as I put the first one on the stage, I knew it was a trilogy,' he said, 'but then I started to see it as more of a series. I was asked to write a new *Mrs Brown* for the 2008

City of Culture in Liverpool, so I suppose until someone says "no more", I shall keep on writing them.

'I could tell you I was a genius and that I knew this was going to be a massive success, but that's not so. What has happened has just been amazing.'

Brendan's celebrity connections helped to boost the annual charity Ward Walk at Our Lady's Hospital For Sick Children at Christmas that year. Brendan brought along his friend Peter Kay, who had been on a visit to his Dublin home, and he stole the show with a rendition of *(Show Me) 'The Way to Amarillo'*.

A marker of what the event means to the kids at the hospital was seen in the case of tragic 16-year-old patient Liam Dunne, who lost his hard-fought battle with leukaemia. A big comedy fan, he was once given the choice of meeting David Beckham or Brendan O'Carroll when those two celebrities were on a visit to Drumlin Children's Hospital. Brendan won hands down.

CHAPTER 23

DEFYING THE RECESSION

By 2009 the global economic downturn was biting businesses hard – and Brendan's business was no different, but he was faring better than most, as he himself observed: 'I'm in comedy and in times of recession people need laughter..

Even though he was noticing a drop in revenue of up to 50 per cent, he wasn't letting it bother him. That old PMA attitude and glass half-full approach never leaves him.

'We're going through a recession, not a famine,' he told the *Irish Sun*. 'I grew up in a two-bedroom house. There were 13 of us. We probably were poor but I had no sense of it whatsoever.

'I am getting hit like everyone else. Sales are down in the UK and I'm getting 35 per cent of a bang off the drop in the sterling, so we're looking at losses of 50 per cent. But if we break even and everybody gets to keep working, it's a wonderful world.

'Thanks to the confidence my mother gave me I have always been a millionaire, without the money.'

And in the spring of that year, there was a new distraction in the O'Carroll household to take their minds of money troubles: a pet duck. His son Danny came across the newly-born wild duckling while playing a round of golf.

Brendan told the *Irish Sunday Mirror*: 'Danny was at the tee for the 17th hole when he spotted all these crows attacking a box that the management leave out for ducks to lay their eggs in. One of them got an egg in its beak and flew off, but it let the egg fall and it cracked open on the grass.'

Danny ran over and saw that there was a tiny baby duckling inside it.

'It looked like it was barely alive and he rang me to ask what to do with it. I told him to wrap it up in a towel and bring it home. The crows kept coming back trying to get it from him and were all around the car when he drove off. It was covered in down and all wet, so I rang my vet and asked him what to do with it. He said that there wasn't much hope but added that they can be surprisingly hardy creatures.'

To Brendan and his family's surprise the baby duck – who they named Donald – began to recover after they dried it off and gave it some water.

Brendan said, 'It's now eating like a horse and has made friends with our two dogs, Fraser and Nialls. Nialls is a big Bernese mountain dog and Donald has really taken with him. I've been told that he probably thinks the dog is his mother! He climbs up on top of him and also pecks at his face. Nialls is very patient with him.

'The duck has now become part of the family and people are constantly calling at the door to come in and have a look at him. It's incredible.'

The duckling loved nothing more than to nestle in Brendan's pocket while he was lying out on the couch and he and Jenny grew so fond of him they couldn't bear to leave him alone at home when they opened their new show at the Olympia Theatre.

'We've decided to bring him in with us,' Brendan said. 'Jenny is organising a cat box for him and we'll leave him in the dressing room. He'll be welcome to stay at home with us for as long as he wants. You should see him, he's the most adorable thing.'

Brendan even wanted to take his new pet duckling to their Florida holiday home – but his plan was laughed off by customs. Brendan said: 'Donald has become a part of the family and we'd hate to leave him behind. But nobody will take us seriously at all when my wife Jenny rings up about getting a visa, licence or passport for him.

'We already have passports for Nialls and Fraser, showing that they have had all their shots and everything, and they're allowed to travel. We just don't know what to do now, as he regards the two of us and the two dogs as his family. I think it would kill him if we left him behind for any length of time.'

Brendan's brand new adults-only one-man comedy show, *How's Your Wobbly Bits?* was going down well with critics and punters alike, giving them three different blasts of comedy – as Brendan's alter-egos of Charlie Smart, a 92-year-old bar room philosopher, and of course Agnes Brown, plus stand-up comedy as himself and out of character.

But he hasn't always pleased the critics and he told Marty Whelan, presenter of the RTE series *A Little Bit Funny*, that he didn't care: 'Do you know, they're the only people who come to the show who don't have to pay. The people who pay into my show night after night – *they're* the critics. When they stop coming I'll change the way I write. The critics can go and kiss the butt-end of my bum.'

And to keep the fans happy and his cast sharp, Brendan revealed to the *Evening Chronicle* how he throws a googly at them to keep them on their toes: 'Years ago, with my very first play, before Mrs Brown, I noticed that after the second or third week, the actors had become really complacent,' he said.

'They knew their lines, they knew when they were supposed to speak, but I noticed they had kind of glazed over. To me comedy is like classical music. It has to be done with passion and if it's not, the audience will spot it.

'It's got to look like you're up there giving it socks, or the audience will go, "They're not really enjoying themselves, so we shouldn't really be laughing."

'So on one of the nights to try to get them out of their glaze, I asked one of them a question that wasn't in the script. Well, it was like looking at six passport photographs. They just stood there in shock. You need to keep everybody on their toes.

'But as it progressed, it's only funny if the audience are

in on it as well because they are paying. What I try to do is keep the play fresh by introducing little bits every night that nobody has seen before. And the cast goes with it. We have as much fun on stage as the audience has watching.'

As well as touring the UK and Ireland, Brendan and family were also trying *Mrs Brown* out stateside, regularly gracing small theatres in New York, Philadelphia and Boston. 'The funny thing is, you really don't have to change it in order to let it travel,' Brendan says. 'You might have to tweak a few of the references. I think Mrs Brown is just a universal mother – maybe a bit rough around the edges – but a mother figure we can relate to.'

In October 2009, Brendan had 'the fifth part of the trilogy' set to debut in Glasgow. This time the action is centred around Christmas in the Brown house, which offered great opportunity for gags and pathos.

'The turkey is getting plucked and Granddad is getting stuffed – or is that the other way around?' Brendan told the *Evening Times*. 'And Agnes is excited because her son Trevor, whom she has not seen in five years, has promised to pay a Christmas visit.

'However, Cathy returns from her trip to America with unwelcome news. But who will tell Mammy? Meanwhile, Rory Brown is distraught because his partner Dino has tried to drown him. As always, Mark and Betty do their best to keep everybody calm, while nobody is sure what to do about Winnie's big box or Grandad's little hamster.'

Brendan said he was unusually nervous about his material this time around, telling the *Evening Times*: 'We are about to stage the fifth in the *Mrs Brown* series of plays and Glasgow will host the premiere of the show. But the problem with that is we haven't had time to run the play in elsewhere. Normally, what we would do is try out a new play in some small theatre in Ireland and then bring it to Glasgow. However, there is so much else going on at the moment this has not been possible.' But the main reason Brendan did not have time to play out of the city was a hugely positive one: *Mrs Brown* was set to become a BBC1 sitcom (more of which in the next chapter).

In the new stage show, the Brown family are beset with excitement, and fear, he told the *Evening Times*. Agnes Brown's son, Trevor, is about to come back from Africa after seven years there as a missionary. Agnes is beside herself. At the same time, there is a dark cloud hanging over the family. It has been discovered one of the brood was adopted – but who is it?

'It is a real family dilemma,' said Brendan. 'Some of the kids are terrified they are not a Brown, but some are philosophical about it.' The play is set at Christmas time, a perfect backdrop for a story about family values, disappointments and celebration.

It would be the 10th year of Mrs Brown's visits to Glasgow.

'The city has been wonderful to us,' Brendan told the *Evening Times*. 'That is why we wanted to premiere the new show here in the city. Mrs Brown and Glasgow are inextricably connected. This city is as much part of Mrs Brown as her cardigan, her thick knicker elastic and the dishcloth that is permanently attached to her arm.

'Although I am a bit nervous about putting the show on for the first time, when you know there are lots of laughs coming up it takes the pressure off. I sit at the typewriter and my wife Jenny can hear me laughing out loud. She'll come in and ask what's happening, and I'll go "you wait 'til you hear what she's doing now". You'd think the typewriter was telling me about it.'

Brendan's old mate Peter Kay popped in to see the show at the Liverpool Empire, which the *Liverpool Echo* hailed as having 'the madness and mayhem we've come to expect from a Mrs Brown outing'.

'"You have to stop crying on my line," Agnes tells flamboyant son Rory (Rory Cowan) before clouting him with a cloth, while Gary Hollywood's camp Dino the hairdresser all but dissolves in the face of a rampant tea towel wielding O'Carroll. In fact there's more corpsing than at any time since the high body count of *Good Mourning Mrs Brown.*'

But as wily Brendan knows so well, constant corpsing, ad-libs and mistakes, intentional or otherwise, are all part of the huge appeal for fans of *Mrs Brown's Boys*.

At the annual Celebrity Ward Walk that year, Brendan revealed that it was the loss of his first-born Brendan Jnr that was behind his support for the event at Our Lady's Children's Hospital in Dublin.

'I was a 19-year-old dad at the time but to this day he remains as real to me as my other three kids,' he told the *Irish Examiner*. 'Patients at the hospital are getting treatments that we adults could not stand. They are taking it on the chin and telling their mothers and fathers not to worry.

'I will be leaving this hospital reassured that we are all going to be OK because the children I see represent our future. Most of the children I see have no idea who I am. You just go in with a friendly smile and ask them how they are doing. I like to try and take their mind off more serious issues, even for just a little while.'

Brendan said he was 'shattered' by the sudden death in May 2010, of Irish broadcaster Gerry Ryan, who had supported his career, and he visited the Mansion House in Dublin, the Lord Mayor's residence, to sign the book of condolence.

'I am shocked like everybody else,' he told the *Irish Independent.* 'We are touring at the moment in the UK so we got home just to do this. The closest thing I can think is of being told when I was a child that Nelson's Pillar was gone. You just couldn't believe it until you see it.

'It is an institution that is gone. He was an amazing help to me. What I was doing was deemed absolutely outrageous. He was always supportive and saying "don't change what you are doing, just be yourself". He is going to be a tremendous loss.'

She had yet to appear on TV but Mrs Brown was becoming a huge hit on YouTube, after uploading a clip of the show filmed at the Liverpool Empire. In June 2010 on RTE's *Saturday Night with Miriam* show, Brendan told how Mrs Brown went viral with more than 2.6million hits.

Many of the hits were from Canadians, so Brendan contacted promoter David Mirvish to set up shows in North America with *How Now Mrs Brown Cow!* in Toronto that August. He was being billed as the 'Susan Boyle of Comedy', as she too had become a global sensation thanks to YouTube.

Unlike his last, unhappy attempt at cracking Canada, this time he would enjoy success, including kinder reviews from critics too.

Robert Cushman of the *National Post* said: 'As we settle in for *How Now Mrs Brown Cow!* a voice, purportedly female, instructs us on the theatre's safety regulations and especially on what steps to take in the event of a fire: "Fuckin' big ones." It's explosively funny, and so is much of the show that follows.'

The reviewer loved the fact that rather than tackle the audience, 'O'Carroll victimises his fellow actors. He's always throwing them off with what we must presume to be ad-libs. You'd think they'd be hardened by now, but I've never seen so many performers breaking up on a professional stage.

'The actor playing the gay son's partner was treated to a succession of slaps, right on his face mic. Trying repeatedly to get his lines out, he was asked, "Are you trying to make a small part bigger?" The audience, myself included, loved it. I especially enjoyed O'Carroll's miming of a tape-rewind to give a cast member a second chance at a line that came out wrong the first time.

'There are any number of faults to be found with the show, and none of them matter. O'Carroll keeps pulling the rug from under everyone's feet, and we all fall happily down.'

And while the reviewer from *The Globe and Mail* didn't like it, she admitted she was in the minority: 'There are two kinds of people in the world – those who love male comedians who don padded dresses and play potty-mouthed grandmothers, and, to judge by the gale-force giggles all around me on the opening night of *How Now Mrs. Brown Cow!*, little, lonely me.

'O'Carroll certainly had fans on hand on opening night whose guts were busting and sides were splitting right from the start.'

Brendan said that, thanks to the YouTube clip, he had also received invitations to take the show to Vancouver, Montreal, Winnipeg, San Francisco, Boston, Chicago, New York, Philadelphia, Sydney, Melbourne and Christchurch.

Brendan, as ever, would make time in the frantic schedule for the Celebrity Ward Walk at Our Lady of Lourdes Hospital for Sick Children back home in Ireland, and by this stage he was organising his annual Florida visits and Christmas holiday plans around it.

He held the two-and-a-half week old child of Gerry and Shannon Curtin from Tralee, Co Kerry, and joked to his son, Eric, who he had brought along: 'You were once as small as that. And look what you turned into – a brat.'

CHAPTER 24

AUNTIE COMES CALLING

To Brendan it had been like any other performance, there was nothing remarkable about it and once again he and his cast had brought the house down in Glasgow – except there had been a very special person in the audience that night.

Eton-educated BBC TV producer Stephen McCrum would have stuck out like a sore thumb amongst the raucous and rowdy Glaswegian crowd. But it didn't take a top level education to see how the crowd was lapping up every bit of the show.

McCrum requested to meet Brendan backstage after the show and thrust his BBC business card in his hand and said, 'Would you be interested in developing this for a sitcom?' He had heard about this foul-mouthed working class comedy that was packing them in up and down the UK and he had to see what the fuss was about for himself. The show was perceived as a perfect fit for a new BBC agenda to bring more blue collar comedy to the network.

'The BBC – Stephen McCrum – he got it,' Brendan told *thefancarpet.com*'s Georgina Wahed. 'And you wouldn't think he would because Mrs Brown is very working class, and he's an Etonian boy, and he got the joke.'

He told Wahed that when McCrum made his proposition, he replied, 'yeah sure' thinking it doesn't work like that, they don't walk in off the street.

'I said, "What do you think of the cast?" He said I don't think you could work with any other cast, they just all know that role so well, and they allow you the freedom to be crazy, you know."

'"Ah, yeah," I said, "so what about the language?"

'He said, "I didn't hear the language, I don't... that's the way she speaks, she's not using the f word as an insult she uses it as an exclamation or a comma." So I was thinking, "Okay, this guy's singing all the right tunes." But still at that time I didn't think he'd get it past the BBC. He was the producer, but I didn't think he'd get it past the higher echelons. And if he did, I thought it's going to be BBC3. But when he came back and said we've got a pilot for BBC One, I actually couldn't believe it.'

The pilot show was filmed at the end of 2009 in front of a live audience in Scotland and would be screened by both RTE and the BBC, as it was a joint production by the two, in early 2010. He told the *Irish Mirror*: 'I actually asked to get RTE on board. The BBC said they didn't need RTE or anyone else involved but I said I would prefer that they were involved from the outset. And I am delighted they came in to do a co-production as now the whole series will run on RTE before BBC viewers get to see it. This is like coming home for us.'

When the TV audience loved what they saw in the pilot and were clamouring for more, Brendan was commissioned for a six-part series. He was told that the BBC regarded *Mrs Brown* as 'up there with *Only Fools And Horses* and *Fawlty Towers*'.

Later, he recalled: 'I'd be shopping in the supermarket with my wife Jenny and I'd stop and say, "We've got a TV series with BBC1!" It's hard to take in, it really is. We're still pinching ourselves to believe it's real.'

And given that his character Agnes was originally created for RTE radio station 2fm, Brendan was thrilled that RTE was also on board for the BBC series: 'It's like the whole thing has gone full circle.'

The TV break would mean that the *Mrs Brown's Boys* stage plays would benefit and prosper even more from the wider TV promotion. 'I'd never give it up,' he told the *Irish Sun*. 'I want to die on the stage. I hope I hit the deck and the audience keep on laughing and think it's the best thing ever. That would make me so happy. I'm in my 50s now but Mrs Brown is 70 so I'll get to grow into the part. I have a great life.'

But there was to be an unexpected potential spanner in the works that threatened to derail Brendan's TV dream – the infamous Russell Brand and Jonathan Ross prank phone call scandal in October 2008, that became dubbed 'Sachsgate'.

There was widespread outrage after the pair phoned

Andrew Sachs, the actor famous as Manuel in *Fawlty Towers*, and left lewd messages on his voicemail, including comments about Sachs's granddaughter, Georgina Baillie.

Brendan had genuine fears that *Mrs Brown's Boys* – featuring raucous antics and peppered with bad language – would be axed in the wake of it. But it transpired that his fears were unfounded. He told the *Irish Mirror*: 'When Jonathan Ross and Russell Brand got into trouble over fuckgate I thought, "Well, that's it, there'll be no series for us."

'I thought they would look at the script and all they would see was fuck and nothing else. But they went ahead with it and we were both surprised and delighted. We got the call in November last year and literally it was a short call and I had hidden a bottle of champagne in the veg drawer of the fridge.

'Jenny my wife didn't know it was there but when the call came from the producer Stephen McCrum I actually thought it was bad news because of his tone. And then he said, "Congratulations, you just have a series with BBC One". I pretended to Jenny it was bad news and I then came in, opened the fridge and got two glasses and said to her, "We're in business."'

Brendan told the *Edinburgh Evening News* that when the BBC first realised that he wanted the series to capture all the anarchy and mayhem of a live show – a cross between a play and a stand-up routine – producers were sceptical.

'I wanted to retain something of the theatre element in the sitcom,' he explained. 'And they pointed out that the sitcom format was invented for a reason. In the end they let me break that reason and think outside the box.' Consequently, in the series Agnes Brown frequently steps out of the action to address the viewer directly.

As Brendan told the *Edinburgh Evening News*: 'There's a scene in which Agnes goes to answer a knock at the door. At that point in the script I just wrote "BOB". That means "bit of business".

'You see, I just know that Agnes will do something on the way to the door – I don't know what she will do because it changes every night, but I know she will do something. I wanted to give the audience at home a chance to see that what they were watching was really happening – we didn't shoot it 20 times to get it right.

'For example, at one point her son shouts, "Mammy, what are you getting involved for? Why don't you just mind your own business!" He slams the door and walks out, leaving Agnes standing on her own.

'As one, the entire studio audience went "aww", I just turned to them and said, "Come on, I'm a man dressed as a woman for fuck's sake." It brought the house down and the camera caught it.

'When the BBC producers realised what BOB meant they went, "oh jeez". In the end all they could do was put one camera on Agnes the whole time. That gave me the freedom to do whatever Agnes would do at any moment.'

The six-part series of *Mrs Brown's Boys* would be filmed later that year to be broadcast the following January, airing on RTE One in January 2011 and in February on the BBC.

By the time the stage show was snapped up for television, the cast was a well-oiled machine made up of close friends and family. Brendan of course is the central cog in that machine. Beside him his second wife Jenny Gibney plays Cathy Brown, Agnes's daughter. His daughter Fiona plays Maria Brown, Agnes's daughter-in-law and wife of Dermot, long played by Paddy Houlihan. A running joke in each episode sees Dermot wearing ridiculous outfits as part of his job in marketing promotions.

Fiona's husband Martin Delany plays Trevor Brown, Agnes's devout son, often away working as a missionary. Brendan's son Danny plays Buster Brady, the loveable rogue and pal of Dermot.

His sister Eilish plays Winnie McGoogan, the next-door neighbour and confidante of Agnes.

Brendan's daughter-in-law Amanda Woods, married to Danny in real life, is also his daughter-in-law in the show but as Betty, the wife of Mark Brown, played by long-time friend of Brendan, Pat 'Pepsi' Shields.

A final family connection is Bono Brown, the son of Mark and Betty in the show, who in real life is Brendan's grandson Jamie. Rory Brown, the camp son of Agnes, is played by Brendan's agent Rory Cowan. Grandad is played by Dermot O'Neill, who has been working with Brendan from the radio show days.

Actor Gary Hollywood, who plays Rory's gay partner Dino, joined the cast after he became pals with Brendan when they worked in panto in Glasgow. The other main recurring character is Maria's meddling mum Hilary Nicholson, played by Susie Blake, plus small cameos for Jenny's sister Fiona Gibney as Winnie McGoogan's daughter Sharon.

There have also been a few cameos by Irish TV and

radio personalities, such as Joe Duffy and Derek Mooney, who are also long-time friends of Brendan. Many of the characters – for example Mark, Cathy and Buster Brady – featured in the original radio series and subsequent best-selling novels. They provided the basis for the plays and TV series but the concept was tweaked and honed – for example, Winnie McGoogan was never in the original works, but was introduced for *Mrs Brown's Boys*.

Initially he considered drafting in celebrity pals like Peter Kay, who he holidays with and had appeared in one of his Mrs Brown DVDs as a travel agent called Jason.

He told the *Irish Mirror*: 'We thought about having celebrity guests in, but we felt the show didn't need it – the whole cast is the same as the stage show and the reason for that is a lot of my family are in it.

'And of course we didn't want to be putting on some-Zthing on television that people wouldn't see when they come to the stage show. I wanted the TV show to have the same characters – the BBC agreed with that, they let me cast it.'

In May 2012, Brendan's sister Eilish told the *Irish Independent* of her emotional journey that brought her through two failed marriages to coming out as a lesbian in her 40s.

It was a decision that came as a shock not only to her happily married husband and two sons, but most of all to herself.

'I was living a very normal life in suburban Surrey,' she explained. 'The boys were on their way to university and I'd a lovely husband. Life was pretty good. What happened came completely out of left field.'

What happened was that Eilish fell in love with a woman. Despite attempts to blame her feelings on a phase or even early menopause, she soon realised they weren't going away.

'Eventually I went to see a clinical psychologist and paid big bucks to be told I was experiencing "transference". He said I had to tell the woman how I felt,' she says. 'I told her, she said she felt the same way and that was it – two marriages, two families blown apart.'

Her ex-husband proved an unlikely source of support and her own family were also accepting. 'Brendan couldn't care less,' she says. 'His attitude was always "if you're happy, I'm happy for you" and the older ones just never mention it.'

And Eilish revealed how she was surprised by how popular the show has become with young and old alike. She told the *Irish Sun*: 'We were all a bit nervous about the TV show. We didn't realise it would be so popular.

'It's great the show is getting the recognition it deserves and Brendan is getting the recognition he deserves. He was never chasing success but it was always going to be a success eventually because that's the kind of person he is.'

Brendan said that at the time of the launch of *Mrs Brown's Boys* on the BBC, he didn't expect the TV show to make him a fortune, but wisely knew it would give Agnes Brown a whole new audience.

'A six-part series won't make you a millionaire but where we will see it is from the awareness raised about Mrs Brown,' he told the *Irish Mirror*. 'We do well in the UK but we have actually never done a gig south of Birmingham. We have everywhere in the north of England and Scotland covered but most of the population is south of there and it might open the door for that.

'We started in theatres holding 250 but now we're playing venues there for more than 2,000 so we have built it up to bigger theatres as well. We have always risked our own money because we produce the show ourselves and it's a hard marketing job.

'But now it looks like we have been asked by a promoter to do an arena tour in June. And we might be able to go to places we have never been before and be sold out before we get there because of the series and people will know who we are. It makes a huge difference workwise.'

Brendan was also thrilled RTE came on board to make the show a co-production and he would finally have his own television series on the Irish channel.

Brendan told the *Irish Sun* in January 2011 that he owed it to Mrs Brown for helping him raise his kids. He said, "It's really weird – it feels unbelievable. I'm over the moon about the TV series. I never thought it would happen so I'm delighted.

'But I never gave up on Mrs Brown. She educated my kids and fed them. This widow with six kids who works in a market stall has bought our cars and our holidays. I owe her everything.

'I'm surprised at how well it travels around the world. One of the books was No 1 in Bosnia at the height of the war there. I get letters from China from people telling me that a Mrs Brown lives around the corner from them.'

The year 2011 would be another defining one in his career

and well he knew it, as *Mrs Brown's Boys* was set to launch on the BBC from 21 February.

Brendan knew that he was onto a winner no matter what. If it failed, well his profile will have been raised further and his stage shows would still be packing them out anyway. His comic talents would also bring him once again the attention of Caroline Aherne, best known from her part in *The Royle Family* and as Mrs Merton.

He had already starred in 2009 as Father O'Flaherty in *The Fattest Man in Britain*, which she had co-wrote. This time she was writing a new comedy programme for ITV called *The Security Men*, and personally requested Brendan for a key role in it as Jimmy, one of four shopping centre guards. Initially thought to be a series, it would eventually air as a one-off in 2013 and also starred Bobby Ball and Paddy McGuinness.

Meanwhile the debate over the bad language in *Mrs Brown's Boys* escalated when it had its first TV outing in Ireland. *The Irish Times* has always been a critic of the sweary nature of Brendan's work, but the row moved to the airwaves and Joe Duffy's RTE Radio 1 talkshow *Liveline* in January.

Joe, an old friend of Brendan's and later to star in the series in a cameo role, was always likely to side with his pal. But he kept it to the facts when they discussed the merits of *Mrs Brown's Boys* and RTE comedy show *The Savage Eye*, with David McSavage.

'All the TV critics and *The Irish Times* love David McSavage and his right-on humour,' said Duffy on the talkshow, 'but they don't like Brendan O'Carroll because he's too mainstream.' Duffy then delivered the coup de grace: *Mrs Brown's Boys* got 760,000 viewers, *The Savage Eye* only 130,000. The public's verdict is the only one that matters to a mainstream figure such as Duffy.

While the profane language may have irked some, there was no denying the figures but also some of the erstwhile themes in Brendan's work.

Brian Mooney, former president of the Institute of Guidance Counsellors, wrote in *The Irish Times* that Brendan had 'performed a huge service to Irish education by handling the literacy issue in a very thought-provoking way in one key scene.

'In the scene, Mrs Brown's son, a plumber, has turned down the offer of a supervisor's position, because he cannot read or write. Amid all the profane language and hilarious laughter, the issue of literacy is handled with huge sensitivity, and will hopefully reach out to many thousands of adults suffering daily from the tyranny of illiteracy.'

The Scottish edition of the *Daily Star* reported that Brendan, who they dubbed the Irish Mrs Doubtfire, had already been commissioned for a second series and a Christmas special before the first series even started.

BBC One had a new agenda to broadcast more 'blue collar' comedies in an effort to recreate the success of classic series such as *Only Fools and Horses*. The channel feared that its programming had become too middle class, with sitcoms about suburban families like *Outnumbered* and *My Family*. So *Mrs Brown's Boys* fitted its agenda.

The changes were being implemented by Danny Cohen, the new, at the age of 36 the youngest, controller of BBC One, who moved from Channel 4 to BBC Three in 2007.

The BBC's Head of Comedy Mark Freeland described the show as: 'A full-on studio audience sitcom starring Brendan as a kind of Irish Mrs Merton.

'In the first episode, Brendan/Mrs Brown forgot his handbag after a scene change, and he/she got up and walked across two sets to retrieve it. We've kept that in – just to nudge the form forward a bit.'

In TV parlance it's called 'breaking the fourth wall' as Brendan explained, talking to Mark Lawson on BBC Radio 4: 'We do it all the time. I deliberately did that [the handbag scene]. The only people that didn't know I was going to do that was the cast. Me and the director had an idea that I would do it – I told him to keep an eye out for that.

'When I'm writing a script, I might write in "Mrs Brown comes in from the sitting room to pick up the washing and heads for the back door. BOB in brackets." That means "a bit of business". That means that between the time she picks up the washing and gets to the back door she's going to do something, I don't know what it is but I just know she will do a bit of business.

'It could be a trip, it could be a stumble, it could be a remark, anything, but she'll do something. And when we had the first script meeting with the BBC boys, they said, "Can we ask, who's Bob and why does he have no lines, he seems to be in it quite a lot but he doesn't have any lines."

'So I explained it was bit of business and there was a little bit of panic when they said "Well, when will you know what it is?" I said when it happens, she may do nothing, and they went, "Oh right, okay, how do we capture that?

'So what they did was, we've got six cameras in the studio and one extra camera that just follows Agnes. That helps the director and it also gives me the freedom to say, "God I've just thought of something, why don't I do it? A BOB."'

BBC controller Cheryl Taylor told *Broadcast* she had high hopes for the show, describing it as 'a bold move' owing to the frequent swearing. '*Father Ted* has sanitised the word "feck" to some degree, and in Ireland it can be used in a much milder way, and I think it would be a real problem if the character were saying "fuck" instead, but it's still a bold move for BBC1,' she said.

'The 10.35pm slot seems right given the language and because Brendan's not that well known. The challenge is in maintaining quality and serving the whole audience, not just people who live in the south or work in the media. We have to be careful not to solely serve our white, middle class, southern viewers.

'Comedy is a hard genre to control, but that journey has begun with programmes like *Mrs Brown's Boys*, and by March you will be able to see a different approach on BBC1.'

Like any good sitcom, Agnes would even have her own catchphrase – 'That's nice!' In the show she jokes that she was taught to say this in place of 'fuck off' while taking elocution lessons.

Brendan told the *Irish Independent* that he knew that at some point he'd be called to a 'fuck meeting' at the Beeb and told to tone down the language, or else. And in September 2010, Brendan was summoned to London for an urgent meeting with Jay Hunt, the former controller of BBC1 who commissioned it.

'I remember saying to my wife Jenny: "This is it. That's the Fuck Meeting."'

But the next morning in London, Brendan was kept waiting 'The meeting with Jay was delayed and delayed, until the BBC told me I wouldn't be meeting her as that day Jay had announced her resignation from the BBC and was moving to Channel 4.

'It was such a big story it made the TV news in Scotland, where Jenny saw it that morning, and thought, "What did Brendan say to that poor woman?"'

Brendan told *RSVP* magazine, 'We had several "fuck" meetings with the producers about how much it's used and regulated. I believe it has a different meaning for the Irish, that it has no rude connotations.

'I was adamant that the TV series reflected the stage show and was representative of it. That said, the BBC occasionally overdub the word "feck" for "fuck".'

Brendan is full of praise for BBC TV producer Stephen McCrum for 'getting it' when it came to tackling the language issue. He told Mark Lawson on BBC Radio 4: 'So what he said to me was, look just do your show the way you would be doing the show, don't be editing it yourself as you're going along and if we need to change an f to a feck, that's what we'll do.

'It has so many different meanings; the f word would be used as a hyphen, as an emphasis. If you were trying to say 65 people were there, you'd say sixty effin five? To mean, more than you expected. But in that context it doesn't mean the f word the way it's supposed to mean.

'And he got it. He got it that it's part of the rhythm of the language, and there are occasions when it just can't be changed. "F off" has a completely different meaning to "feck off".'

Brendan spoke out in defence of Mrs Brown's coarse

language when he appeared on Gay Byrne's *The Meaning of Life* interview programme (RTE): 'If Mrs Brown says 20 pounds or 20 f-ing pounds, does it matter? Really?

'Does it matter? I think there are a lot worse four letter words than the f word, I think rape is worse, I think kill is worse. You know, what Mrs Brown says is funny. F doesn't make it funny and taking out the f won't make it less funny. It's funny.

'The woman I have in Mrs Brown is an authentic woman, she's not something I made up, she's absolutely authentic and for me, taking the f word out or the feck out, the buck out of any of her stuff, to me would be like taking every second word out of a Wordsworth poem and think it would still have the same rhythm, it doesn't.

'And if you notice on the TV series, nobody else says it. Not one other actor on that stage says the f word, only Mrs Brown. Do you know why? Because she wouldn't have bad language in her house. And that's Mrs Brown.'

The blue language in *Mrs Brown's Boys* was predictably an easy target for the tabloid media, and after the TV show's launch, the *Express on Sunday* got the ball rolling with the headline 'BBC show uses f-word 34 times in 30 minutes'.

They said it was a record number for BBC1 but that the station was defending the show, and indeed a BBC spokesman countered: '*Mrs Brown's Boys* is a bold and confident new comedy series for BBC1 with warmth and humour at its heart. The language within it is very much part of Mrs Brown's vernacular. The series has been very carefully scheduled way past the watershed at 10.35pm and the content will be clearly signposted for viewers.'

Producer Stephen McCrum added: 'It is refreshing for the BBC to find something that is so blue collar. BBC1 controller Danny Cohen has been talking about the non-middle class sitcom and the need to find them. I always try to find stuff that otherwise wouldn't be on.' Asked about the language, he argued, 'I think it's completely authentic to the character that she speaks in that way.'

Brendan told the *Irish Sun* that the language was no big deal. 'I don't even see them as curses. When we originally made the series, it was for the BBC and there's only two ways you can have a popular Irish show in the UK.

'It's either a *Darby O'Gill and the Little People* show, which is not me, or it's a rock'n'roll style Bob Geldof, and that's definitely more us. I can understand if people are genuinely offended but thankfully that's why they made a swinging door in theatre and why they invented the remote, you can turn it off if you don't want to watch.'

Brendan discovered he had won another new celebrity fan, when *Little Britain*'s Matt Lucas tweeted that the show looks 'bloody hilarious'. He said: 'It's a great boost to hear that. The tweets so far have been great, and I probably should thank the general public first because they pay the bills but you do get a bit of a buzz when you hear people like Matt.'

He would be one of many. Footballer Joey Barton is a big fan. He tweeted after a later episode: 'The missus was nearly in tears there. Mrs Brown on the tablets... funny show that. LOL.'

Brendan couldn't believe it when 870,000 people watched the last episode of *Mrs Brown's Boys*, in Ireland beating the *Late Late Show*.

Never has a new show divided so much opinion and

provoked so much comment and debate as when *Mrs Brown's Boys* finally made its debut British TV on Monday, 21 February 2011, much of it centred, predictably once again, on the swearing and bawdy humour, key elements which fans of the show lap up, of course.

The critics, armed with a preview recording of the show, sharpened their pencils two days before it aired. The Mr Marmite of comedy would delight and infuriate them, not that he would give a monkey's and, if anything, was probably delighted by the publicity.

The Daily Telegraph called it 'an old-fashioned blend of silly voices and slapstick, played out in front of a live studio audience who collapse into giggles at the mere mention of the word "willy". O'Carroll won't care what the critics say – the show's already topped the ratings in Ireland.'

The Guardian called it a 'fourth-wall-smashing sitcom starring... an interfering, gutter-mouthed mother-of-six - the TV version of a hilariously rude stage show', adding, 'we're rarely more than 20 seconds from a "feck", or the more common Anglo-Saxon equivalent – although even the clean one-liners are often pretty wonderful ("When I was 18, I married his son, because of a condition I had called pregnancy").'

The Independent made it their Pick of the Day and said 'Subtle? No. Funny? Quite.' Yet *The Scotsman* savaged it, however, calling it an 'atrocity'. Their critic wrote: 'Evidently the winner of a cruel wager to write the worst sitcom known to man, it stars inexplicably popular Irish comedian Brendan O'Carroll as his foul-mouthed alter ego Mrs Brown, an irascible elderly matriarch for whom no single-entendre is too weak to resist.

'Having peddled this charmless character for years onstage in his homeland, he's somehow convinced the BBC that a shrill, lazy, desperate and depressing TV version should be inflicted upon the entire UK.

'Although performed in front of a studio audience, it boasts a robotically tweaked laugh-track quick to cackle at every F word and things that aren't so much jokes as words delivered in an ostensibly comedic way.'

The Times said the fact that it had so many real-life family members might 'explain why it exudes such warmth and good humour'. They added: 'It's not a show that you would go to in search of subtlety or insight, but it is fast and exuberant and exploding with energy, and everyone – cast and audience alike – appears to be having the time of their lives.'

Sister paper *The Sunday Times* said: 'Like *Mrs Doubtfire* after a crate of Guinness, it's "feck this" and "feckin' that", as his Irish matriarch blunders round her home and relationships. It is broad, old-fashioned humour, delivered with energy.'

The *Sunday Herald* wrote: 'The most interesting aspect of this TV version is that, as in the good old days, it's filmed before an actual live studio audience (who we occasionally glimpse) in an attempt to replicate the raucous feel of the theatre performances.

'The show itself is almost mesmerisingly awful, though, trapped in a sub-Lily Savage meets Roy Chubby Brown-lite furrow that's not so much old-school as just old. Unless you like it, of course. In which case, it's probably feckin' brilliant.'

The *Daily Record* likened it to a combination of 80s

sitcom *Bread* with Catherine Tate's Nan in the central role. They said the 'brilliant comedy' was 'laugh-a-minute stuff' before adding, 'but it's perhaps best avoided if you're offended by swearing, because Mammy Brown uses the F-word so often even Gordon Ramsay would admit defeat.'

The Herald (Glasgow) said: 'Is this for real? Brendan O'Carroll takes his stage show on to the small screen and it's really, really bad. I mean, truly awful. And it's going straight on to BBC1! It's a signal. I'm telling you. The end of the world is nigh. It must be.' Equally negative, *Metro* found it 'jawdroppingly past its sell-by date', and added 'the BBC should hang its head in shame.'

Yet *The Times* loved it, quoting the script: *'I'll need a sample of his urine and a sample of his stool,' requests the doctor. 'What did he say?' mumbles the patient, Grandad, as daft as he is deaf. 'He wants your underpants,' responds his daughter-in-law, Mrs Brown.'*

The Times' critic went on: 'The above quote comes from the piercingly funny *Mrs Brown's Boys*, in which the Irish comedian Brendan O'Carroll drags up as a fecking-and-blinding middle-aged mammy.

'When she's not accidentally Tasering herself in the neck with a safety alarm, she's deliberately breaking the show's pretence: "It's a man in a fucking dress," sighs O'Carroll when the studio audience shows sympathy for the old bag. Far from being as annoyingly frenetic as it sounds, what stands out is its comfort in its own skin, its naughty spirit and its good heart.

'Most of all it does something that few sitcoms now seem wont to do: stacking itself with brilliantly tight, imaginative gags. Mrs Brown's affectionate dig at her daughter, once a flat-chested teenager: "I was going to get you glasses at the time so people would know which way you were fecking facing." Fecking good stuff.'

He was dividing the critics more than ever but Brendan was delighted that the first episode had pulled in 2.64m viewers – about one in six of all viewers at the time – an above average audience for the 10.35pm slot. 'I'm completely overwhelmed with those figures.'

And Tam Cowan of the Scottish *Daily Record* leapt to his defence, claiming that rival critics should 'take the poles out of your bahookies, boys, and stop slating the wonderfully funny *Mrs Brown's Boys*. Yes, it's a bit dated, a wee bit rough round the edges and one or three of the jokes were probably first cracked in Victorian times.

'But it's good, harmless fun and the studio audience – not to mention the viewers at home – clearly love it. Three bits this week meant I was like a hyena on laughing gas.

'Mrs Brown urging her neighbour Winnie not to buy a Labrador as "loads of their owners end up going blind".

'The crossword clue in her puzzle book – constipation, seven letters, begins with "n" and ends with "n" – that she eventually decided was: "Nnnnnnn!" And if you didn't even smile at Mrs Brown's DIY bikini wax, well, you must be dead.'

Talking about the success of *Mrs Brown's Boys* on TV in an interview with presenter Stephen Nolan on Radio Ulster's *The Stephen Nolan Show*, Brendan said: 'I have to tell you, it's a bigger success than I ever thought it would be. People are coming up to me at the moment and saying, God you must be living the dream. To be quite honest Stephen, I'm way past my dream. I passed my dream a long long time ago and it's going into the realms of fantasy at this stage.

'I think we're providing a need that's very definite out there, you can feel it, people just need a laugh, and the show's providing a laugh and it's as simple as that. I don't think it's any more complicated than that.

'The difference the TV has made, let me try to put it in perspective for you from a monetary point of view, we would do... I only work 26 weeks a year, I set that out when I started in this business, I only work 26 weeks a year and I take 26 weeks off, as life is too short to be working your life away.

'In that 26 weeks the company would turn over, prior to the TV series, maybe £1.5/1.6million. After the TV series you're looking at us turning over between £8 and £9million. It's that huge difference it makes.

'And really what it's done is it's become a calling card. In order for us to break a city like Liverpool with the shows, there are five live Mrs Browns, we would have to go back three times to that city before it would catch on.

'We're now going to cities that we've never visited before and they are already aware of the show, and it's already selling out, so it's a phenomenal success on all levels, and it's also quite a personal success, in that when you sit down and write these things to sometimes 4am or 5am in the morning and you're wondering what you are doing with yourself, you think that people are going to enjoy it, or you hope that people are going to enjoy it, and from a writer's point of view it is just amazing, when you hear people laughing at a line you wrote, inside you're saying, that's what I meant when I wrote this.

'The success this time round means it gives me as a father an opportunity to see the future of my kids more secure, not secured but more secure. I'm very lucky and they are very lucky, Fiona is an excellent actress and Danny is an excellent actor, and they've got great futures ahead of them in the business.

'And I can't make them good actors, I can't get them a part, I can certainly help them get an audition, and what they're doing now will get them an audition for many, many things.

'But they've got to go and get that themselves, for no other reason than I wouldn't deprive them of the adventure of going to get it, it's a great adventure, the trip is the fun, not the destination.

'So what's next and where does the success go? I don't know, but I know it'll be a new adventure. And having looked back and talked about the movie and the ups and downs of it all, it has been, and I knew it would be when I started in this trade, a rollercoaster ride. But God almighty – what a ride.'

At the same time *Mrs Brown's Boys* was winning new fans across the UK, Brendan took *Good Mourning Mrs Brown* to Toronto. He joked to the audience that promoter 'David Mirvish had promised him that it would be a cold day in February before he was ever allowed on a Mirvish stage again'. So here he was.

His curtain speech had the audience in stitches, but the Canadian critics were not feeling the love second time around, however.

The Globe and Mail said, 'Mrs Brown has been

welcomed back to Toronto with open arms by her fans, but will no doubt be greeted again with crossed arms by critics. My hands remained tucked under my armpits for most of *Good Mourning Mrs Brown*, anyway.'

The *Toronto Star's* reviewer wrote: 'As I sat at the Princess of Wales Theatre on Wednesday night, watching the premiere of *Good Mourning Mrs Brown*, I felt like I was having an out-of-body experience. All around me, I could hear people laughing, but in the whole 160-minute show, I only cracked a smile twice.'

And Robert Cushman of the *National Post* said, 'I have to profess myself disappointed and, in view of my previous enthusiasm, more than a little shamefaced. It seems safe to say that when you've seen one Mrs Brown play you've seen them all. It's probably worth seeing one though.'

But as Brendan always says, his audience are his real critics, like readers of the *Scottish Daily Record* who wrote to its letters page: 'With all the news of doom and gloom, what a tonic to forget it all watching *Mrs Brown's Boys*. 'It's brilliant and better than any of the so-called other comedies we get these days.' (Frank Rice, Dundee.) 'I watch *Mrs Brown's Boys* on BBC1 and the tears of laughter are great in these times of recession. The show takes you away from everyday problems.' (E C Wishaw, Lanarkshire).

And there-in lies a big reason for the success of Brendan and Mrs Brown – escapism, an opportunity to forget about the 'doom and gloom' of the recession and real life.

Three weeks after it made its British TV debut, *Mrs Brown's Boys'* ratings continued to rise, drawing in an extra 500,000. 'It's a bit overwhelming,' Brendan told *The Scotsman*. 'It's the first sitcom with an 85 AI rating, I have no idea what that means but people seem really fucking impressed by it.'

And as for the language? 'I thought it was only fair to the audience that what they saw was a fair representation of what they would see if they came to the stage show. The last thing I wanted to do was do a sanitised version of Mrs Brown and have a nice audience coming to the theatre and saying, "Holy Shit what it this?" But the BBC supported us all the way.

'We shoot it from start to finish without stopping. I wanted it to have a raw edge. It's old fashioned-style comedy, but with a modern edge and it makes people laugh out loud.'

In March it was confirmed officially that the show had been commissioned for a second series.

It was also announced that *Mrs Brown's Boys* had been nominated in the Best TV Comedy category at the prestigious Monte Carlo Television Festival Awards.

Only Brendan would have the bottle to advertise in both Celtic and Rangers programmes for his stage show in Glasgow, but so loved is he in the city that it was a shrewd move to film his series at the BBC's Pacific Quay studios there.

Brendan explains, 'They also gave me a choice of where to film – Manchester, London, Belfast or Glasgow. The very first time I played Mrs Brown outside of Ireland I played at the Pavilion in Glasgow. The city has been very kind to me and I knew we would have an audience.'

In April, Brendan told the *Daily Star* which plots from his hit plays would make it into the second series on TV. He said: 'I haven't actually written a fecking word. I think I have it mapped out in my head but I don't know where I'm starting or where I'm ending.

'Agnes is stuck in the 70s and 80s with her values so I think it's time for her to go cyber. I want to introduce a couple of things that would be new to her or that she hasn't done for a long time – one being the computer and the other that she should get her leg over.

'I can't believe how it's taken off. It's old-fashioned and it's meant to be. I only write comedy that makes me laugh. People seem to love the mad bitch.'

He also told the *Liverpool Echo*: 'Basically I'm doing what I've been doing for many years, but I think it's just a question of timing. We're in a recession and people are a bit down, so they need a laugh and traditionally comedy always does well in a recession. But in this particular case, people also get nostalgic. I think it's a very old-fashioned sitcom. The timing just happened to be right for us and people are loving it, thank God.'

At the same time Brendan was pushing forward with tour dates, taking *Good Mourning Mrs Brown* round the UK and Ireland again, and he couldn't believe the news at the end of April when he was told that *Mrs Brown's Boys* had been nominated for a Bafta in the Situation Comedy category.

He told *The Irish Times* he was 'gobsmacked' to be listed ahead of the likes of the *Inbetweeners* and *Miranda,* neither of which were nominated.

CHAPTER 25

A BAFTA? THAT'S NICE!

The early signs were good – very good – when it came to the all-important viewing figures for the second series in 2012.

The first episode of the second series of the comedy was seen by an audience 6.61million (28.2%) when originally broadcast at 10pm on 26 December, according to the TV industry Barb figures.

But consolidated figures, adding those who recorded and watched the show within a week of broadcast, handed the comedy an extra audience of 1.63m, the biggest boost of all shows broadcast on Boxing Day.

This took its total audience to 8.24m (30.4%) and made it the fourth most-watched show of the day. In addition, it was double the previous biggest audience of 4.1m (23.5%)

that saw the series one finale, broadcast on 28 March 2011.

In his native Ireland, Brendan was performing well in the ratings too, his sitcom was the most-watched TV show in Ireland over Christmas with a viewing figure of 880,000 viewers, a 48.6 per cent share.

More movie work came in the form of the small-budget, straight-to-video Irish production of *Scrooge*, in which Brendan starred as a secondhand merchant called Old Joe. The movie starred pals of Brendan's like Bryan Murray, who he worked with in *Sparrow's Trap*, and comedian Brendan Grace.

The family experienced real-life drama during their break in Florida that year, when Brendan's 28 year-old son Danny saved a man from drowning when he pulled the victim from a pool and resuscitated him. Brendan arrived at the scene just as paramedics did, not realising that is was his lad Danny who had dragged the hefty Asian pensioner from the water and resuscitated him.

Danny, who has a house alongside his dad and sister Fiona in the Florida gated community, later told the *Irish Mirror*: 'People are saying I'm a bit of a hero but I think anybody would have done the same. Of course [Brendan] was proud as punch of me when he heard the details. He gave me a big hug and told me I had done really well.'

In February 2012 Brendan battered 'Golden Balls' and Jonathan Ross in Britain's weekend TV ratings.

The BBC had previously been screening *Mrs Brown's Boys* on Monday nights, but bosses decided to go for the big one and switch to Saturday to see how the programme fared against heavy-hitter Ross over on ITV.

The final episode of *Mrs Brown's Boys* showed who's

boss – beating chat icon Wossy by 2.4million viewers on Saturday night. Even an appearance on Ross's couch by David Beckham couldn't outscore Mrs Brown. The public voted with their remotes and 6.32million tuned in to see Mrs Brown provide the laughs.

The Jonathan Ross Show kicked off with Becks and actress Keira Knightley on ITV half an hour earlier, but only managed to hold on to an audience of 3.92million.

Brendan said, 'It's just the perfect end to the series – wow! I just heard from the BBC that the overall consolidated figure, which includes Sky+, is looking at over eight million.'

Speaking from his holiday home in Florida, where he was outlining scripts for the next series, Brendan told the *Irish Mirror*: 'It feels like all this is happening to somebody else. It doesn't seem real. We knew the last episode had to be moved from Monday night, as it's the Queen's Jubilee, but I was very nervous when I heard it was going out on Saturday night – and against Jonathan Ross.

'I firmly believed that the opposite would happen and he'd trounce us. To get a 29.5% share is just outstanding. I got the news at 6am yesterday and I've been up ever since. The BBC also has a thing called an Appreciation Index, where a selected audience vote for their favourite shows that week.

'The record used to be 83%. Then for the past three episodes we had 91%, 91% and then 92% – which a BBC comedy has never reached before. We haven't got the AI in for last Saturday yet, but I hope it will even beat that. The very first episode drew 2.4million viewers and we were delighted with that. We were thrilled. But this is just astonishing. It's unbelievable.'

When Brendan jetted home from his Florida holiday the night before the IFTAS (the Irish Film and Television Academy Awards) he headed straight for his friend Louis Copeland's tailor shop to get kitted out with a €35 hired tux and acid green dickie bow – and was all set for the big night.

Accompanied by his wife, Brendan revealed he was working on a new project for HBO about which he will say nothing 'in case it doesn't work out'. But Brendan was excited to be in the running for an IFTA. 'There is something about being recognised in your own country that is really special,' he told the *Irish Mirror,* and he was delighted when *Mrs Brown's Boys* took home the IFTA for Best Entertainment Programme, taking a swipe at critics.

He said, 'I don't care about the people who don't think it's funny. I just say, "Fuck them". That's why we designed remote controls. When people are down and not well, they need a laugh.'

The Late Late Show host Ryan Tubridy presented Brendan with the award for *Mrs Brown's Boys* which he said made him laugh 'like a drain'.

He told the *Irish Mirror*: 'I am a big fan of *Mrs Brown's Boys*. It is a phenomenon – look at what it does in the ratings. 'It is one of those programmes that is the *Fawlty Towers* of its generation in the sense it's got that weird appeal.'

Tubridy believes the show is getting huge ratings as viewers need cheering up in the midst of economic misery. He added, "I think it is the anti-recession programme. People are sick of Sarkozy, they want Brendan O'Carroll. They're sick of the news – look at the figures for the news bulletins, they're really low. People are so depressed. They want something else, they want warming up.'

The second series bowed out on a high with consolidated figures for its finale of 8.3 million, vindicating the BBC decision to move the last episode of the series onto Saturday night.

The sitcom by this stage had already been commissioned for a third series and had sold a million DVDs since October 2011, making it the BBC's third fastest-selling comedy debut after *Little Britain* and *The Office*. Brendan joked, 'I'm thrilled to see one million DVDs go out of the stores. But I'm running out of places to store them!'

At the end of February, Irish comedian Hal Roach – a great inspiration to Brendan – died at the age of 84. The Waterford-born entertainer, who was known for his catchphrase 'write it down', died in Florida. Brendan, who was so moved by his death that he wrote a 700-word appreciation in the *Irish Independent,* said Mr Roach was 'tremendously encouraging to the other comedians he met... He gigged all over the world, flying the Irish comedy flag. Thanks for the laughs Hal. You will not be forgotten. Not in this house.'

Brendan first saw Roach perform when he was a 17-year-old waiter at the Green Isle Hotel and described him as 'the Arthur Askey, the Les Dawson, the Eric Morecambe of Irish comedy, all rolled into one'.

Brendan's ability for diversification with Agnes over the years has known no bounds, but still he would conjure up new outlets for her. From radio to books to the stage and TV, with cinemas on the radar as well. And in March 2012 the *Irish Independent* revealed she was now set to go global in an animated cartoon.

Brendan revealed that audiences from Brazil to Japan will soon hear the Dublin housewife talking in their own language, thanks to a new cartoon series. The co-production, between Universal Studios and Mr O'Carroll's own production company, had been planned for four years.

'I always knew that if I could get Mrs Brown on to BBC TV, it would explode. So about four years ago I started a project in Arizona where I put a team of animators together to turn Mrs Brown into a cartoon series,' Brendan explained.

The animators' work can already be seen on the opening credits of the BBC series *Mrs Brown's Boys*, which features Brendan's character at her washing line. Brendan said to raise the profile of the cartoon, he got the BBC to use the cartoon caricatures that the animators had created.

Just when it looked like things couldn't get any better or bigger for Brendan O'Carroll, it was revealed that *Mrs Brown's Boys* was being made into a multi-million-euro movie.

The *Irish Sunday Mirror* reported that two major studios were fighting to buy the rights to the hit comedy which could be on the big screen as early as next year (2014). According the paper, the movie will have a €10million budget and Brendan stands to make at least €2million.

Speaking to the newspaper from his Florida home, Brendan said: 'Universal Pictures and Canal Plus, a French company, are vying for the rights to make a movie of *Mrs Brown's Boys*. I'm thrilled at the interest, no matter who makes it. It's perked up the whole family.'

Brendan also told *Daily Star Sunday* that he was lining up Anjelica Huston and Tom Jones for his movie, quoting him saying: 'Universal and the BBC have given us the green light on the film. We begin shooting in October next year with a release date of May 2014 scheduled. I have already done the outline of the script.

'In the original film Anjelica Huston played Mrs Browne and I had a small role as a tramp so I'm thinking about casting her as a bag lady in the new film. I haven't asked her yet but I will do. We are still in touch and I'm sure she will.

'Tom Jones was also in the original so I'd like to have him back in some role as a cameo. It would be nice to go full circle and give a nod to the original film. But that's it. I don't want the movie to be about getting famous faces in it for the sake of it. That's not what the show is about.'

The *Irish Sunday Mirror* also reported that Brendan had signed a whopping €3.5m deal with the BBC for a brand new comedy series based on his previous hit play *The Course,* as well as agreeing on storylines for the final series of *Mrs Brown's Boys* which will see the star's grandson, Jamie, having a part in the show playing the character Bono.

The paper quoted Brendan saying that the pilot of *The Course* will be made later in 2013: 'It's so funny, I remember the people in the Dublin Theatre Festival telling me it wasn't up to the standard they required and it went on to outsell everything else they had on. I'm really looking forward to making it. Instead of the original six characters, we'll probably make it a dozen for the TV series, along with special guests. And I will definitely use my manager Rory [Cowan] in *The Course*, although he may not play a gay character this time around. We'll see.'

Rory Cowan told the paper it was sweet justice after they were knocked back the first time they tried to stage

The Course back in 1995 and instead put up promo posters with 'The Play Rejected By The Dublin Theatre Festival', which pulled in punters by their thousands.

The Course will star Brendan's wife Jenny as a demented housewife, son Danny as 'Stuttering Tony' and his daughter Fiona, who plays a demented prostitute. Brendan, of course, will play the lead character again, Joe Daly.

In April *Mrs Brown's Boys* was nominated for Best Comedy series at the 52nd Monte Carlo Television Festival. Brendan and Jenny were also up for best actor and actress awards and the show had two production nominations. It is already huge in Iceland, South Africa and Romania. But it's set to go global after the rights to the first series were sold to the US and the rest of the world.

Brendan told the *Daily Star Sunday*, 'I honestly can't fucking believe it. It really is crazy to think it's blown up so big after years of doing it. After the success of the TV show people approached me about the animation, which will now be distributed across the world and translated into numerous languages. I'm in the middle of two huge tours, which have sold out, and the DVD is doing so well too.'

He was adamant that he wanted to move on from TV, bar Christmas specials: 'Series three will definitely be the last. Even if the next series gets ten million it's still time for me to stop. What a great high to go out on.'

On 24 April 2012 it was announced that *Mrs Brown's Boys* had picked up three Bafta nominations for best situation comedy, where it would face Channel 4's *Fresh Meat* and *Friday Night Dinner*, and BBC2's *Rev*.

Brendan meanwhile was up for best male comedy performance for his portrayal of the often puerile Mrs Brown. He was up against *Spy*'s Darren Boyd, Hugh Bonneville for his performance in *Twenty Twelve* and *Rev*'s Tom Hollander. Director Ben Kellet was nominated for his role in the show.

The programme received one nomination the previous year but was pipped to the post but now after hitting big ratings after going primetime, Brendan was hoping this year would see a Bafta on his mantelpiece.

He said, 'I'm gobsmacked but thrilled. I have tummy cramps already, but I'm sure the same happens to Meryl Streep.'

The show was such a hit it had been sold to The Comedy Channel in the US and is now been shown in Canada, South Africa, Australia, New Zealand and Iceland.

Brendan said the Bafta nominations were the results of 20 years of hard work, especially at the beginning when the show struggled for acceptance. 'It is nice to see the critics finally catching up,' he said.

And then, of course, Brendan's finest hour came on 27 May 2012 at the Royal Festival Hall in London when *Mrs Brown's Boys* won the Bafta in the Situation Comedy category. Ecstatic, Brendan fought back tears after winning the prestigious honour, and he brought his cast and crew on to the stage to share the moment.

He told the star-studded audience: 'All we wanted to do was make people laugh and it seems to have worked. I want to thank Steve McCrum who walked into a theatre in Glasgow four years ago on a rainy October night and saw us work and said that's comedy or maybe *that's* comedy? We're a bit pleased; we have brought the family. This is amazing. All we wanted to do was make people laugh and it seems to be working.'

Rory Cowan said the cast was still on a high days later following the awards ceremony and said that Brendan had already chosen the exact spot in his home for the award: 'He has an awards cabinet and it's getting the best spot in it – right beside the IFTA.'

Gary Hollywood told the *Daily Record* the award was like giving two fingers to the TV snobs: 'We have taken the blows along the way and we are especially pleased for Brendan. The public have always been with us, but the critics have been hard on us and Brendan would have to take the bad reviews on the chin.

'We have come full circle, got over the rough times and we are over the moon. We were up in the same category for situation comedy last year and lost out. That was another blow. Of course, you want to win, so for it to happen this year is phenomenal. We are so chuffed.

'I was sitting shoulder to shoulder with the likes of Jennifer Saunders, who is a huge fan of the show. She was delighted we won and said it was fabulous to have such great comedy on the telly.'

Brendan told the *Irish Mirror* he was 'proud as punch' of his family after their hit show bagged a Bafta. He said: 'I'm still pinching myself. Jenny and me just look at each other and giggle. I am so proud to have stood on that stage with a Bafta in my hand surrounded by my family. We have worked so long and hard for this and on Sunday night the gods were with us.'

The delighted cast and crew celebrated their win at an after-show bash in London's owish Langham Hotel where they were partying until the small hours. And a delighted Brendan promised his Bafta would make its first 'live appearance' on tour, as Agnes intended to shine up her award on stage, starting with the first live show of *Mrs Brown's Boys* at Cardiff's Motorpoint Arena in June 2013.

Reflecting later, Brendan said that his life had 'flashed before his eyes' as he took to the stage at the Festival Hall for the awards ceremony. Speaking to Ryan Tubridy on his 2fm show, Brendan added: 'It was an Obama moment – I was walking down there going, "My God, yes we can!"

'On the walk down to the stage my life flashed before my eyes – I was thinking about Billy Flood, the teacher I had when I was 12 years of age who introduced me to reading. He set up a little library in a Tayto crisp box. There were 44 kids in the class and he brought in his own books and put the two hardest kids in charge of the library. So you brought your books back or you'd get done.

'And the first book I took out was *Treasure Island* and it took a long time to read it because I am a very slow reader, I still am now. It just took me to a different world.' Brendan said he took out the book time and time again so when he left Mr Flood had a present for him.

'When I left school he wrapped the book in brown paper and handed it to me. He said, "Take that with you wherever you are going". And I still have it. He was an inspiration to me. All of those people right along the line flashed before my mind as I took to the stage.'

And Brendan admitted he was glad Mrs Brown got the

gong for Best Sitcom even though he personally missed out on the Best Actor award. He said: 'Those people standing behind me have worked on the live show and there were weeks that they worked with no wages because it wasn't there to pay them. And this was their day.

'We waited a long time for this and it was like I made my Holy Communion, Confirmation and had Christmas morning all in one day.'

The team between them took four Baftas including all the technical awards. But Brendan admitted he doesn't take any of this for granted. He said: 'I am glad to be working, we have always worked hard. But as well as that – look at my life, this is a privilege.

'I was a waiter for 18 years and any time I think I might be getting tired, I think, "You know what, I could be standing outside the Ashbourne House Hotel waiting on the wedding to arrive and knowing I am going to be working until 3am."

'Friends of mine are coalmen, and when it rains they would be delivering coal on their backs for the whole eight hours of the day and when they finish, nobody will clap. I am privileged to have the life I have and I remember that every single moment.

'For an Irish show to take the award in the UK there was something special about it. Entertainment-wise we have always boxed well above our weight and I recall many people talking about the 80s European Championships and how it changed our attitudes to ourselves as we did feel more confident.'

Even though he said winning the Bafta was vindication for him and his supporters, the comedian admitted on Ryan

Tubridy's 2fm show he still gets wounded by a bad review: 'You get 150 great reviews and one stinker and that is the one that ties a knot in your stomach. I don't know why we do it but we give that more weight than the good ones. And I have to say to people – if I can do it, anyone can do it.'

What also meant a lot to Brendan was receiving letters from the parents of more than 100 autistic children saying they had heard their child laugh for the first time because of Mrs Brown.

'I will fund the research if there's anyone out there who can do research into this,' he told Ryan Tubridy. 'There has to be something in it. That's the eraser on the end of your pencil that rubs out your critics.'

Brendan told the *Irish Daily Mail* more about his plan: 'When the first couple of letters came in, it made me smile – but when hundreds came in, I realised something was happening. Mrs Brown seems to be making a connection with these children. I am getting letters from parents saying they had never seen their children laugh before but when they watched the show they were laughing out loud for the first time.

'And I am sure it's not just my show. Charlie Chaplin and Buster Keaton could also have a real impact on these children and comedy could help tap into their laughter. We need to look into this because it is worth more than all the money in the world to me. I want to fund this research to see if comedy could do something for autism.'

CHAPTER 26

THE BRENDAN WE KNOW

'If I knew what it was, I'd bottle it and sell it,' says Brendan about the secret of his phenomenal success. He might not know what it is, but what about those people who have seen him at close quarters, why do they think this unlikely working class Irishman has become such a worldwide success story?

I spoke to four of the people who have worked with him at close quarters across his two decades in show business to get an insight into 'the man who is Mrs Brown':

Adele King is an Irish entertainer – better known by her stage name Twink – who has known and worked with Brendan for years. 'He has funny bones and that's what we call it in the business,' she says. 'The real bottom line on it is that funny is just funny.

'So many comedians nowadays, I feel a lot of the new alternative comedians, God they have to work so hard to be funny. Stop working so hard. Stop going up and down the stage at 100 miles an hour.

'You see, Brendan makes it look effortless. And he's a funny little huur. He didn't think, "I'm going to be a comedian." He was always funny, as long as I've known him. And he's got a very sharp active brain. If you've ever watched him do the after-show thing with the audience, it's funnier than the show.

'He has these one-liners for the audience that come out just spontaneously. Some people say funny things and other people say things funny. He just has funny bones, you can't be taught it.

'It doesn't have to be a gag per se, he has the oldest gags in the world in that show but he revamps them and puts them into a sitcom situation.'

Adele believes that Brendan became a hit in the UK in particular because men in drag have always been a hit there through the years, from Les Dawson to Dame Edna Everidge.

'It's the old fashioned old dames and the reason it took off in Britain is because, unlike us here, and thanks be to God for my career in panto, but they don't have panto dames here now.

'I grew up working with Jimmy O'Dea as the dame and Danny Cummins, and that was phased out here. But in Britain they still love their big television star men playing Widow Twankey and playing the dame part.

'They love men dressed up as aul wans, it's always been a penchant of the British. And I think he just fell right into that, with the aul wan with the big boobs hanging over the table and the aul rollered hair and the neighbours and the cup of tea, it's almost like a kind of a piss-take of *Coronation Street* isn't it?

'It's the comings and goings of an average family down the pub, in the kitchen – it's so uncontrived, it's about everyday life and eccentric old characters like Grandad.'

Adele says she remembers clear as day the first time she saw Brendan do stand-up and he had the audience crying with laughter.

'I just think that Brendan has always been funny,' she says. 'I remember going to see Brendan in the Rathmines Inn. We were all doing a television show together at RTE and he said "I'm on in Rathmines" and we all said "come on we'll go down to see him" and we all barged into the pub.

'Honest to God I was going to sue him, because I aged 20 years that night, I had so many lines on my face the next day, I never stopped laughing from the time he came out on stage. And there was no Mrs Brown or anything then, it was just Brendan O'Carroll and band.

'He is a force of nature. I just think some people are just very electrically wired and they exude electricity from them, even within the cast, he is a centrifugal force that all the rest of the comedy works from him as the hub of the wheel, going outwards from him.

'In a lot of sitcoms, a lot of the comedy in them can be balanced in favour of one and then when the other comes into the scene it's their comedy piece.

'But with Brendan it most definitely comes from Brendan, he is the centrifugal force of the comedy, it all emanates from him.'

Adele says she also admires Brendan's tough stance on

standing by his cast, his writing and his refusal to sanitise or change anything from his hit plays when it came to the TV series.

'It helps the fact that he writes it and compiles it as well,' she explains, 'and I know from him that he had arguments, I think even with doing that thing at the end of the show.

'The wonderful thing about Brendan is that he's a little terrier, he's a little ratter, he's a Yorkshire terrier and he's just stood by his own beliefs and said "no, this is part of it".

'And of course it's been a resounding success. He has an innate good sense of what works. I just think he's a funny little huur, he's just one of the funniest guys.

'I remember one night we were on the *Late Late* together years ago, it was Pat Kenny's time, we were in the VIP room and we were sitting there and the tears were running down our faces. We could not stop laughing.

'Brendan doesn't need anybody else, he's a one-man band, Australia now have gone mental for him, and I hear he's turning down telephone numbers from companies in America to do cartoons and he's holding on to the rights and rightly so.'

Adele thinks that the fact that Brendan came into the business late – and learnt valuable financial lessons along the way such as *Sparrow's Trap* – means that he can appreciate success second time around.

'He was very wealthy once before and he lost it all,' she points out. 'It was rags to riches back to rags. That was a great lesson for him. You can see how the poor young kids like the Justin Biebers and the Britney Spears of this world go off the rails, because they're too young to handle that kind of success and money.

'But when you've had your fingertips burned badly and you've known what it's like to be rich and then back to being poor again, I think that's a very salutary lesson.

'I mean, he's a very bright man, I think he's taken good stock of what it's like to have it and lose it all. However, I don't think he ever had as much as he has now!' she laughed.

'But I would wish him nothing but success because I love him dearly, we've been on the circuit together, we're around the same age and he came later into the business than I was, I was in it from childhood.

'I found a picture of me and him the other day in the house of us at a charity do and I just thought, "Ah Brendan, I'm so delighted for you." I would wish him every success and may he conquer the whole world.

'And do you know what? I want to say to his detractors and all the begrudgery – listen, all of the people all of the time cannot be wrong. You can't tell people what to laugh at.

'People can decide for themselves and they have decided. They have decided the vote is thumbs up. It's funny and also his use of the f word is brilliant because when he comes out with it you're not expecting it and I think he has done that very cleverly.

'I think anybody that says it's a load of trot needs their head examined. It's good old-fashioned laugh out loud – LOL! My daughter has introduced me to this "LOL" culture and his life story could be called LOL – laugh out loud because that's what you do with him, you laugh out loud.'

Tommy Swarbrigg was Brendan's promoter for years, including the early days of the *Mrs Brown's Boys* plays.

'I promoted him for a few years around the country when he was doing stand-up and then also I did the first plays with him,' says Tommy. 'He and I and Gerry Browne co-produced them.'

And Tommy points to Brendan's incredible self-belief, ambition and natural talent as being the secret to his success: 'He's a complete and utter natural. He talks incessantly; he was always ideas, ideas, doing this, doing that.

'He would always drive the people with him. When I was with him, he would absolutely convince you this was 1,000 per cent going to work.

'And of course, he is a very funny guy, and stuff comes out of him all the time. We spent long nights at hotels drinking coffee and chatting and having the laugh, and in his house as well.

'How would I put it, he has complete self-belief and the first play he did was *The Course*, it was terrific. That was a huge success, he and I and Gerry Browne produced and put it on all around the country, we even brought it to Britain.

'The second thing was a play called *Grandad's Sure Lily's Still Alive*, I remember begging him not to do it and of course we lost all the money we lost on *The Course* on that one. And then he did *Mrs Brown's Boys* and again that became a huge success and then after that we went our separate ways.'

Tommy said the bad experience of trying to crack Canada with *The Course* followed by the aftermath of *Sparrow's Trap* proved too much for him but that he is not a bit surprised by Brendan's soaraway success now.

'We had brought *The Course* to Toronto and it was a very gruelling experience and very hard with the language

250

in it, they just didn't seem to accept it, and I was bone weary after that. I spent a good bit of time in Toronto pushing it and I just opted out but we remained friends.

'But I'm not a bit surprised by his success; he always completely and utterly believed he was going to make it. It went down terrifically well in Liverpool and the reviews were ecstatic and the punters absolutely fell around the place laughing, so that was the start of his international career.

'The stand-up which was unbelievably funny, it petered out simply because it was just a little bit too blue, so we were losing repeat customers and then he started writing the books of course and they were a huge success.

'And I was with him there alongside him all the time and I said "brilliant". He could also paint; I said "yeah paint and we'll put on exhibitions".

'He could turn his hand to most things. His books were very well written, simple and full of laughter and sold in their thousands, No 1 on the bestsellers list.

'He never really failed at anything, apart from *Sparrow's Trap* and that was where he and I parted company. That was part of the reason, I just didn't have the money to put into that so I opted out of that. That was exactly when I left, at the start of *Sparrow's Trap*.'

Tommy said the failure to get the six-figure tax exemption grant – the Section 35 certificate – for *Sparrow's Trap* hammered the nails into its coffin: 'It failed to get the tax exemption and it was completely based on that, you had to get the tax incentive to get the investors in to put it on.'

But he is delighted by Brendan's success now and says he is equally not surprised to see his family members and former agent Rory Cowan starring with him in *Mrs Brown's Boys*.

'He kept telling me "you could be an actor, anybody can do it". And of course he now has his entire family in the thing. I actually played a part one night when we were stuck; I played one of the parts. "Come on now you can do it, of course!" he said to me.

'So I went up on stage and did it as well. He makes you believe you can do it, absolutely. He has complete self-belief and that permeates down into those working with him.'

Gerry Browne, an accomplished folk musician, helped Brendan break into the entertainment business and the pair became on-stage partners as Brendan's showbiz career took off like a rocket.

'We grew up together in Finglas and we did great,' he says. 'I had a folk band from Finglas called Tinker's Fancy and we used to play in Brendan's pub. Brendan had the lease with another guy on the pub, and the pub was in trouble, it was a place called the Finglas Castle.

'We were gigging in the pub and we were the only band at the time, because we were local, with a local following. We'd have a big crowd. I remember the first night we were there he came over and said "Jaysus, youse are a great band and blah blah blah."

'I said to him, "Is that because you think we're good or because we bring a big fucking crowd?" And he said, "No, no a bit of both." He was very charismatic. We ended up doing every Sunday night.'

Gerry revealed that Brendan's real stage debut was when he was still running the pub and Gerry encouraged him on stage one night: 'One of the guys didn't turn up one night for some reason and we were struggling a little bit time-wise to do the full set.

'So I'd also been in his company when he'd been telling a few gags and I talked to him and I said, "Listen, would you get up and do a fucking spot?"

'And he said, "ah you're joking" and I said, "go on" and he got up and I have to tell you, he had the place in uproar. Brendan is the best stand-up comedian I have ever seen or heard in my life. He got up on stage and he tore the place down. The following Sunday we did the gig and he did the same again.

'And then the place went bang, the place went down for a couple of reasons. Him and the partner had split, there were a lot of debts.

'So I kind of approached him and said, "Look, why don't you come gigging with us? Because I think this could really grow." So we started gigging together, himself, meself and another guy. We started a thing called *Blind Date*, we'd get people up and it was very, very different.

'It was run on the basis that the music was good, but the comedy was brilliant. He'd get up and do some gags and then we'd play *Blind Date*, but the following came within a very short space of time.

'We got a huge following on the Dublin pub circuit and I was kind of managing the act, as in booking the gigs and fighting the publicans over the money. And in a very short space of time we'd become successful and it went from there, we took a chance and we went to a guy called Pat Egan.

'And Pat had put us into the Tivoli Theatre with the stand-up show, which was much the same show that we had been doing in the pub. And then all of a sudden things just took off.'

Gerry told his version of how things escalated when they landed the spot on radio and revealed that he had been begging *The Late Late Show* to give them their chance.

'It was shortly afterwards then that we kind of blagged our way into RTE with *Mrs Browne's Boys* the radio show. The producer went on holidays and we'd given him the script, it was done in five-minute episodes for 2fm and a guy called Gareth O'Callaghan's show.

'The producer said, "Ah man, this is fucking rubbish." So we ended up that when he went on holidays, thanks be to God, Gareth took a risk and at this stage we were a four-piece band and we had a four-piece road crew and a guy at the door taking the money and it ended up that with the eight of us that we got *Mrs Browne's Boys* the radio series up and running.

'And of course, there was no money in it, it used to cost us money to do it, to record it, but what it did was, it gave us national exposure. And then we took off around the country doing the show, the stand-up.

'Brendan's wife had breast cancer and I'd been trying to get on *The Late Late Show*, I'd been ringing them and sending them stuff for well over a year they just wouldn't take the risk.

'But then the story, the angle that was used, was Doreen's cancer. And believe it or not, that's how we got onto that very, very first *Late Late Show*.'

I asked Gerry if he thought he was responsible, in the nicest sense of the phrase, for creating a monster by encouraging Brendan to try his hand as a stand-up.

'I'd put it to you like this, in some ways I am, but Brendan is an immense talent, he's an amazing guy. Even though Brendan isn't the best singer in the world it didn't stop him singing on stage. He had this great positive mental attitude; he believed in the whole PMA thing.

'When the pub closed down that time he was in dire straits, he was in absolutely dire straits, he would often say, "Jesus man, thanks be to fuck you came when you did" and you know it goes both ways.

'Although I wouldn't say I was very wealthy but I was never stuck for money, I had a good job and my own business and we went out on the road then, Brendan was a great operator now I have to say.'

Gerry marvels at how huge *Mrs Brown's Boys* has now become, remembering well all the ups and downs they shared on their rollercoaster journey together.

'Do you know the funny thing about it, we had been on the road for so many years, we used to go to the States and Canada, we were doing pub gigs and then Brendan wrote the play *The Course*.

'The great debate at the moment that's going on, people say to me "your mother is Mrs Brown" and we would have written a lot of stuff in the kitchen, me mother's kitchen.

'I'll let Brendan answer that one, I know the story has changed, it used to be based on my mother but I think since we parted company that that's not only the case and it's based on other people, but you know, that's poetic licence.

'I mean there were some really, really tough times; there were times when him and I, I ran the band and ran the show etc and for a long time we wouldn't get paid, the lads in the band got paid and the road crew got paid.

'The live show was quite rude, it would have been a cross between Chubby Brown and others, and people would go "Oh my God it's so rude." We deliberately went that road.

'We did *The Mammy* together, I was one of the producers of it; I'd lost my part in it because I broke an ankle six days before shooting.

'We had *Sparrow's Trap* previously which caused an unholy mess. I'd invested a lot of money in it, when *Sparrow's* went down and still the debts were hanging over us, I think at one stage it was IR£2.4million we owed between us and it was a nightmare of all nightmares.

'I borrowed IR£660,000 off friends and family, even people I didn't know I borrowed money off.

'We were desperately broke after we did *Sparrow's Trap*. One day my wife Colette told me I had missed nine of my son Aaron's 12 birthdays and I decided to leave after the movie, *The Mammy*.

'My daughter Sarah was five or six and I had become very disillusioned with the entertainment business. I had remortgaged twice to fund various projects and when *Sparrow's Trap* went south I was bankrupt.

'Brendan's financial situation from then is well known but we were both severely burned by the movie industry – I spent years paying off my side of things. I had enough really and decided I didn't want to do it anymore.

'But I didn't think *Mrs Brown's Boys* would become as big as it did. To be honest with you, we had done all the tours then we done all the plays together on the road with Mrs Brown and I knew it was big, but I have to say as much as we were big, to transfer it to TV I think was a stroke of genius by Brendan, I have to say now.

'And it's funny, we only talk about it now, some people hate it, some people love it, if you don't like something you don't watch it – that's all you do.

'But the success of it is phenomenal. It's amazing. I'm delighted for him, I really am, he's a great worker Brendan; he's a phenomenal worker.

'We would have been very urban, I suppose a bit rough around the edges. I remember Tommy one time describing us. "Jaysus" he said, "they're very talented, but they're as rough as a bear's arse!"'

Gay Byrne is truly a legend in Ireland, as the host of *The Late Late Show* and a raft of other hit programmes since. He is credited with launching Brendan's career proper after giving him his chance on the biggest show in the country.

'Well obviously we saw something in him then, he wouldn't have been on the *The Late Late Show* if we hadn't seen something in him then.

'He was just starting out and the first time he was on he was extremely funny and he done extraordinarily well and everybody loved him and all of that.'

Gay believes that Brendan is a modern-day exponent of the old vaudeville acts and has earned his success after years treading the boards with his act and building his reputation.

'He is so steeped in show business anyway, so steeped in old-time vaudeville and it seems to me that *Mrs Brown's Boys* is nothing more or less than continuing in the great vaudeville tradition, going back through Maureen Potter and Jimmy O'Dea, and don't forget Biddy Mulligan the Pride of the Coombe.

'And before that there was Cecil Sheridan and then going right back to an old vaudeville character called Old Mother

Riley. The vaudeville tradition is men dressing up as daft aul women and coming on stage and doing daft things.

'And Brendan O'Carroll would be the first one to say that that's exactly what he's doing. He would be the first one to tell you that he's doing nothing now on BBC television or RTE television that he wasn't doing in the Olympia Theatre for the last 20 years and completely ignored by television people who thought on RTE and BBC that what he does is rather infra dig and they wouldn't have put it on television.'

'And now he's the hit of the season and is remarkably successful and it's a show that is quite clearly travelling all over the world.'

Gay believes that Brendan's indefatigable ambition – even though not always getting it right over the years – is the driving force behind his huge success now.

'He's come up with some daft ideas, he wanted to start his own airline at one stage and run a 727 around to Donegal – completely potty, but he's allowed these type of things.

'He has huge ambition and he has huge ideas of doing great things, so you forgive him all of that because I think he's going to be funny for the foreseeable future.

'I think he's going to be busy doing what he's doing for the foreseeable future, because it is eminently successful. I suppose fashion comes in comedy and television programmes like everywhere else, whether it is shoes or shirts or ties or suits or whatever.

'Fashions change and we've had so much of the sitcoms, American, Australian and British that this is a whole new thing that got off the ground.

'Somebody had faith in it just as years and years ago somebody had faith in a thing called *Fawlty Towers*, there were people even at that time in the BBC who read that script and said "this is a disaster and it should never see the light of day and it's going to be a hopeless failure" and they were proven totally and completely wrong.

'In the same way somebody somewhere thought, "We'll take a chance at this, the Brendan O'Carroll thing *Mrs Brown's Boys*."

'The surprising thing is that the level of bad language in it and foul-mouthed effing and blinding, that would have been unheard of on RTE television or BBC television five years ago, four years ago, three years ago.

'And the only surprising thing about it is that he has made a breakthrough, given that there is that amount of obscenity in it, but everybody seems to love it and the Americans seem to think that everybody in Ireland talks like that and they think it's an Irish brogue when we know it's Dublin and nothing like an Irish brogue.

'But there you are, he's a terrifically successful guy, I'm extremely fond of him, he's extremely fond of me, we were together for a little meal a short time ago and he was in the best of form.'

The over-riding theme from all who know Brendan is his unshakeable confidence and self-belief, but like Adele King, Gay also points to the fact that Brendan is also a man of principle.

'He sticks rigidly to them,' he says. 'The amazing thing is that he got some amazing offer from American television just recently and he turned it down because he wants his 26 weeks on and 26 weeks off.

'And that's clear cut and that's his and that's a wonderful thing, he's not allowed himself to be wooed by the offer of colossal money.

'And of course one of the most other amazing things about him is that the entire cast is made up of members of his own family and they're all terrible actors but they enjoy it and it's great skit and it's fun and long may it last.'

Brendan's manager and stage sidekick Rory Cowan has also played an important part in the comedian's success story, and has his own views on what makes the man tick. He told the *Irish Independent* that Brendan is blessed with a phenomenal memory which allows him to rattle on unscripted for hours on end: 'The first time I saw him he was doing 90-minute regular shows on a small circuit. You can't go out there week after week recycling the same material, so he was changing it from show to show.

'So by the time he did his first *Late Late* he had five or six shows' worth of material memorised. I've been with Brendan for 20 years and the critics have never liked him but the people have always loved him.'

Rory said that from the very first moment he saw him in action he realised that Brendan has had an understanding and appreciation of both his own audience and his own worth.

'I was putting on rock acts in the Bottom of the Hill pub in Finglas, but one week I had to fill a gap so I booked in Brendan. He wanted IR£400, which was a lot of money then, but I paid him his asking price and made IR£1,400. The next time he asked for IR£700 and I agreed straight away. I just added IR£1 to the admission and still did really well.'

That underground success continued unabated, with Brendan taking Britain by storm and by stealth – the north of it anyway. Rory explained: 'We are a huge draw from Birmingham to all points north. South of Birmingham you couldn't give our tickets away.

'But that's because in London they want a six-month commitment to staging a show and we're far too busy and in demand to give that amount of time to building an audience we don't need.'

While Rory is Brendan's manager, he insists the comedian is very much his own man: 'It's him that does it all. He manages himself. He has an instinct for what the people want. He knows how to re-invest himself.

'When it came to creating Mrs Brown we thought the role would be played by an actress, but she didn't show up. So Brendan just slotted in the voice thinking it would be re-recorded. But someone said that's great and he took on the part.'

Rory says that while Brendan's natural sharp-witted ability as a comedian is testimony to his talent, it is that unshakeable self-belief, the gospel according to PMA, which is the real key to his success: 'He has this gift of mind over matter. Every time he's been given a kick in the bollocks he's picked himself up and started over again.'

As RTE's head of comedy in the 1990s, Billy Magra mulled over giving Brendan O'Carroll his own show back then, but it didn't happen. 'It was a different zeitgeist,' he told the *Irish Independent*, but that didn't diminish his admiration for Brendan's never-say-die attitude.

'There were years when Brendan didn't have a

broadcaster and he would put his hand in his own pocket to fund his end of year show.

'He'd stage the production and film it and then put it out on video and DVD, and it would sell,' he says.

Without a broadcaster in the late 1990s, Brendan noted with satisfaction that his self-financed videos sold a quarter-of-a-million copies.

'There can't be a quarter-of-a-million fucking eejits out there,' he remarked.

His unfailing willingness to take a punt on himself is rooted in the born gambler within. In bygone days he flitted away fortunes at Shelbourne Park.

'I was mad into the dogs,' he recalled. 'The first three times I went to the dogs I won big. On the third occasion, I was only 13, I had five shillings and I won IR£815. I thought "this is easy". Big fucking mistake.

'I was hooked and it got worse as I got older. I used to get off the bus at Shelbourne Park on a Saturday night after getting my wages.

'I'd walk to the bus stop where you got a bus back to town. I'd lift the sod at the bus stop and put a 50p piece under the sod so that at least I'd have my fare when I came out. I knew I was going to lose my bollocks.'

He packed in the dogs and focused his gambling bug on a single project – Brendan O'Carroll. As Billy Magra summed it up: 'He's done it himself. He's a one-man cottage industry and you can't take that away from him.'

CHAPTER 27

MRS BROWN TAKES OVER THE WORLD

With a raft of awards to his name – the pinnacle of them being that Bafta – where will Brendan go from here? Well they can only get better.

The TV ratings have got higher and higher. In turn, his plays have moved to arenas, and he is selling out shows more than ever before.

That is making him a fortune, as are DVD sales and all sorts of other merchandise. Mrs Brown the brand had become a juggernaut.

The third series of *Mrs Brown's Boys* won the lion's share of the audience between 9.30pm and 10pm with an audience of 8.1million (29.8%), adding more than 2million viewers to its 2012 series debut.

In fact, *Mrs Brown's Boys* was watched by an incredible

38million viewers over Christmas in total in the UK and Ireland, by far the biggest show over the festive period.

It topped the ratings in the UK on Christmas Eve and Boxing Day and was the most watched programme In Ireland on Christmas Day as well.

And Brendan celebrated a bumper Christmas after *Mrs Brown's Boys* also trounced Michael McIntyre in the DVD sales. 'We did it,' he yelped. '*Mrs Brown* is the UK Christmas No1 DVD in every chart. Yippie.'

Brendan even gave his old friend, RTE presenter Joe Duffy, a cameo as a psychic in the third series. 'I've known Brendan for 15 years now,' Joe told the *Irish Mail on Sunday* as he gave an outsider's insight into how the shows are made and what goes on behind the scenes.

'I've always supported him. He used to make movies himself years ago, he was a director and he starred in them. He made feature-length DVDs when he was struggling. I played a priest in one of them about 10 years ago.'

Joe said that Brendan called him out of the blue a few months before filming started to tell him he had the perfect part for him in an upcoming episode of *Mrs Brown's Boys*.

'He rang me early on in the year when he was writing the script and he said he had a role going for a psychic. Now, he knows me, he knows I have no belief in psychics whatsoever. If anything, I'm always trying to expose them,' Joe said.

And so keen was Joe to appear in the hit show that he appeared for free – even taking three days' leave from his job at RTÉ radio.

'I did it for free, it's not like I'm a Hollywood movie star, I'm just Joe Duffy,' he said. 'I took three days off to go over and do it and it was a great education and I do what I can to support Brendan, that's it. The minute he asked me, I said "yes".

'It's pretty strict, the whole process. There's eight cameras, everyone has to know what they are doing next. It's not a stand-up comedy gig with one fella standing on the stage for 90 minutes. It's a big coordinated operation.

'There is such a massive cast – in the one episode I was in, there were 30 people in it. I have to say it was really hard work. They were a long three days. I'd say it's one of the biggest studios in both Ireland and the UK. They had the three locations set up in the one studio and it was filmed live in front of about 500 people. They filmed it twice; and each filming takes three hours. So I was on from three to six and seven to 10.

'The day I was filming, people had come all the way from Australia just to be in the audience. And even though people had come from all over the world to see it, like from Ireland and Holland, even though their tickets had been allocated months beforehand, they still all queued from nine in the morning to get the best seats,' he said.

Joe said it was just as much fun off-camera, joining the cast and crew at Brendan's place after filming. He said, 'Brendan organised a table quiz in his apartment – I thought it was just for one or two of us to have a bit of a laugh, but every one of the crew turned up.'

Joe, who like Brendan has inner-city Dublin roots, said he firmly believes that Brendan's success is all down to the man himself and he couldn't be prouder.

'Brendan is just great. Because he writes it too, he knows every single line, he knows the way he wants you to say it, he's great,' Joe said. 'And he has a Bafta award-winning crew around him, including directors and lighting directors. Some of them come from Oxford, they have incredible CVs and they love working with Brendan O'Carroll, they really do. They absolutely love him.

'We have no idea here of the true phenomenon that it is. It is worldwide at this stage. The critics here [in Ireland] don't rate him. It beat every other show last year, the audience is just stunning.

'It's great to see an organisation like the BBC putting so much into the show. Nothing is left to chance, it looks like it's haphazard but it's nothing like that. The floor manager is one of the best in the UK, the director has a number of Baftas.

'I think it's so successful because the show is built around the family, there is a sense of protection there,' he said.

Robin Ross-Thompson from the *Daily Dispatch* newspaper in South Africa revealed that he couldn't get enough of Mrs Brown on YouTube and was calling for it to be screened there too.

'They're an absolute hoot,' he said. 'They're a riot and I can't wait for the series to start here.'

It was a sign *Mrs Brown's Boys* was looking set to go global again with more and more channels around the world seeking the rights to reproduce it.

'We are exploring every avenue we can with her,' Brendan told *TV Now*. 'And currently we are doing a pilot of *Mrs Brown* out in Arizona. We have put an animation of her together, which means we can now do it in other languages.

'And I also sold the character rights for TV to Romanian TV, Lithuanian TV and Czech Republic TV. Now the

Romanians are running it at the moment with their top comedian playing Mrs Brown.'

With Brendan filming the movie in 2013, there would be no *Mrs Brown's Boys* going into 2014, although both the BBC and Brendan were delighted to announce there would be the Christmas specials which he would commit himself to until 2015.

In January 2013, Mark Freeland, BBC's Head of Comedy, said: 'Last Christmas, Agnes Brown was stuck halfway up the Christmas tree. This year in every way she will be the star at the very top. I can't wait.'

And Brendan added: 'I'm thrilled that the BBC has asked us to be part of its Christmas again this year. It's a great privilege to be invited into people's homes at such a magical time of year.'

As well as shooting the $6m movie, provisionally titled *Mrs Brown, De Filum* (although Brendan also like the name *Mrs Brown D'Movie*) at Shepperton Studios in August, Brendan and co would be beginning a tour in March.

But he flew in from his Florida holiday home in January 2013 to present an award at the UK's National TV Awards at the O2 in London, at which *Mrs Brown's Boys* had been nominated in the Best Sitcom category – and won.

Brendan thanked fans of the show and made a joke about having so many family members involved: 'The only person that's not in the show is my mother and that's because she is dead,' he said.

He also thanked the voting public, saying: 'All of you at home, you've no idea but you've changed all of our lives, thank you so much.'

He told the *Guardian* afterwards he was finding it hard to fathom his own success; 'To not be able to get from the check-in to the aeroplane without stopping for 40 photographs is really weird,' he says. 'I don't even think my mother if she was alive would want a fucking photograph of me. Analyse this and tell me what the secret is, 'cos I don't have a fucking clue.'

As if he doesn't already have enough on his plate, Brendan is also looking at a *Mrs Brown* spin-off. Like the banter with the audience after the show, it would allow him to combine the character with his natural ability as a quick-witted stand-up with a host of sharp put-downs up his sleeve.

He has also filmed a pilot for a new TV game show for the BBC called *Mrs Brown's Celebrities* and said the stars were in stitches. If given the green light, the *Celebrity Juice*-style show would be geared for a primetime Saturday night slot.

He told *TV Times* in January 2013: 'Basically it's Mrs Brown taking the mickey out of famous people because she doesn't know who they are. We shot a pilot episode with Kate Garraway, Robbie Savage and Russell Grant and they were crying with laughter.

'It might make Mrs Brown a bit more famous but we can't get any more people into the gigs than we already do. I was weighing it up and commercially it makes no sense but watch this space.'

The *Irish Examiner* revealed Brendan was considering a u-turn and would consider a fourth series, but only after his movie was released in 2014. He said that winning another award at the NTAs, and it being voted for by the public, forced his hand.

Speaking at the awards he said: 'I always said from the outset to my producer Stephen McCrum that it would be three series and that would be it. But it's been so successful and brought in so much money, that we will do the movie this year, which we start shooting in September.

'It's called *Mrs Brown D'Movie*. That should be in theatres in June next year to compete with the World Cup. Once we've finished that there may possibly be a fourth series. I certainly didn't think I would be as fond of it after three series as I am. I thought I would be a bit tired and a bit fed up.'

He joked: 'We didn't do it for the awards, we did it purely for the money!'

He added that his live tour had sold 250,000 tickets by Christmas. 'With that kind of response, you really do want to go on,' he said. 'We do it for the audience, I don't want to write something that somebody in such and such newspaper would like.

'I can only write what makes me laugh, and what makes me laugh is the comedy I grew up on.

'You write what makes you laugh and as a writer you hope that the audience agree, and so far they do.'

Brendan told *The Sun* in January 2013 that *Downton Abbey* star Hugh Bonneville was being lined up for the movie and that the plot would see Agnes take on a syndicate wanting to build a shopping centre where her veg stall is. The foul-mouthed Irish mammy is defended in court by a barrister whose career suffered due to his uncontrollable tongue.

Brendan said, 'This barrister hasn't represented anyone for five years because when he is under pressure he develops Tourette's. I'm hoping to get Hugh Bonneville for the part. I wrote it with him in mind and couldn't stop laughing – I think he'd be brilliant.

'The movie will revolve around a court case after a politician, developer and banker team up to close a Dublin market. They think Agnes's stall will be easy to shut down because she's a widow – but she has no intention of going anywhere without a fight.

'She employs a solicitor, who her daughter Cathy falls for, and a barrister – which is where Hugh will come in.'

BBC producer Stephen McCrum was equally stunned at the success of the show and said it was a godsend, after he went to see it only three years previously on the recommendation of friends, including *Rab C Nesbitt* creator Ian Pattison.

'I went along to see the show,' McCrum told the *Guardian* in 2013. 'And it was very, very funny. I don't believe in God, but I nearly did that night. The audience was full of 200 old women laughing, alongside ushers who were about 16 or 17 and also pissing themselves. It was immediately clear: there's something happening here.'

And Brendan's collaborators on *Mrs Brown's Boys* say the natural family atmosphere, because so many relatives are involved, as integral to the sitcom's success.

'It must be one of the few programmes,' says director Ben Kellett, 'on which, every week, the first 10 minutes of rehearsal is given over to hugging.

'The entire cast comes on and hugs the entire crew. Every single person who works on that show knows all of the cast's names, and the cast knows all of the crew. And that is a very unusual thing.'

But to Kellett the real secret of the show's success is Brendan himself. 'He has a very good knowledge of comedy,' says the director. 'He's massively self-critical. He's hugely driven. He's got incredible energy. He's naturally and emotionally intelligent as well as being comedically intelligent. It's a great range of gifts.'

And McCrum compares him to Leonard Rossiter. 'To have that control of an audience, it's extraordinary,' he says. Others reference Buster Keaton yet Brendan names everyone from *Cannon and Ball* to *Are You Being Served?* among his influences.

'I have absolutely no problem recycling old gags,' says Brendan. 'The old is new if it hasn't been seen for a long time. And y'know, every time we have a new child, we tell them the same fairytales we were told when we were kids. And they sound great!

'Who gives a fuck? It is what it is. There are people who will love it, and people who won't.'

Brendan says the people who love it are 'the audience that comedy forgot' as modern-day alternative comedy took over.

'It's got a confidence in itself, and a joy,' says Kellett, 'and a harmless revelling in the downright silly'.

'It just works,' adds Stephen McCrum. 'People want a good solid laugh, and they want reassurance that everything's all right.

'Brendan delivers emotion, comedy, great performances, and he delivers a nice world to be in on a Monday night when you might be a bit fed up at the start of the week. You can criticise that as much as you like, but it works.'

It hasn't just worked, it has soared. It has been every bit as incredible as Brendan's rise to the top itself.

He was born into a poor family; working class; left school at 12; dyslexic; worked at all sorts to try and make a crust, mainly a waiter for 18 years.

He suffered heartache, most notably the loss of a child; a divorce; depression as he stared bankruptcy in the face. But he had one thing that enabled to withstand all that – self-belief; PMA.

He found love again. He became a worldwide success as a comedian, a novelist, a playwright, a radio star, a TV star, a movie star. His talent knows no bounds.

His is truly is a rags to riches story. The man with the Midas touch.

So surely he'd have few regrets and couldn't wish for anything more?

Only one thing.

That his dear mum Maureen was alive today to witness and share in her boy's phenomenal success.

When Brendan stood on stage to collect his first Bafta for the phenomenally successful comedy series in 2012, it marked a new milestone in his incredible career that is still continuing to grow.

But he dearly wished his mum had been there to see his finest honour.

'My mum would have loved this,' he said. 'When I was a kid she used to tell me that I could be anything I wanted to be.

'And I believed her, it gave me great confidence but I remember once saying to her, "Well, I can't fly."

'But she said, "Yes you can. All you have to do is put your arms out, and I promise you, one day you'll take off."

'And I swear to God, when I stood with that Bafta in my hand, I just wanted to say, "Look Ma, I'm flying."'

A few years back, in uncharacteristically philosophical mood on Gay Byrne's *The Meaning of Life* interview programme (RTE), Brendan tackled the question, 'What's the meaning of life?' His answer was:

'To make sure that I leave a footprint. I was born and I will live and I will die like everybody else, but to make sure I leave a footprint that makes a difference and that means two sons that are good enough to be somebody's husband, a daughter that some husband will be proud of, and grandchildren that will look some day at DVDs or re-runs on television and go "that's my grandad".

'That's it.'

SOURCE MATERIAL

Adele King – interview with the author
Allentown Morning Call
Birmingham Mail
Boston Herald
Broadcast
Canberra Times
Daily Dispatch, South Africa
Daily Mirror
Daily Star
Daily Star Sunday
Daily Record
Edinburgh Evening News
Evening Herald, Dublin
Evening Mail, Birmingham
Evening Times, Glasgow

Express on Sunday
Finglas – A Celebration, Aidan Kelly, Finglas
Environmental Heritage Project
Finglas: A People's Portrait, Samantha Libreri, New Island
Fresh Air, Nation Public Radio, USA
Gay Byrne – interview with the author
Gerry Browne – interview with the author and pictures
Highland Radio
Hobart Mercury
Hot Press
Independent News & Media (pictures)
Irish Daily Mail
Irish Mail on Sunday
Irish Mirror
Irish News of the World
Irish People
Irish Sun
Irish Sunday Mirror
Mark Lawson, BBC Radio 1
Liveline with Joe Duffy, RTE Radio
Liverpool Daily Post
Liverpool Echo
Los Angeles Times
National Post, Canada
National Public Radio, USA
Newcastle Evening Chronicle
Newcastle Journal
News of the World
Northern Echo
Orlando Sentinel
RSVP

Saturday Night With Miriam, RTE
Scottish Mirror
Scottish Sun
Sunday Business Post
Sunday Night, Channel Seven, Australia
The Daily Telegraph
thefancarpet.com
The Guardian
The Globe and Mail
The Herald, Glasgow
The Independent
The Irish Examiner
The Irish Independent
The Irish Times
The Late Late Show, RTE
The Mammy, Brendan O'Carroll, O'Brien Press
The Meaning of Life, RTE
The Scotsman
The Stephen Nolan Show, Radio Ulster, BBC
The Sun
The Sunday Herald
The Sunday Independent
The Sunday Times
The Times
Tommy Swarbrigg – interview with the author
Toronto Star
Tubridy, RTE 2fm
TV Now
TV Times
Wicklow People
Would You Believe, RTE